Black Indian Genealogy Research

African-American Ancestors Among the Five Civilized Tribes

An
Expanded Edition

Angela Y. Walton-Raji

HERITAGE BOOKS
2018

HERITAGE BOOKS
AN IMPRINT OF HERITAGE BOOKS, INC.

Books, CDs, and more—Worldwide

For our listing of thousands of titles see our website
at
www.HeritageBooks.com

Published 2018 by
HERITAGE BOOKS, INC.
Publishing Division
5810 Ruatan Street
Berwyn Heights, Md. 20740

Heritage Books by the author:

Black Indian Genealogy Research:
African-American Ancestors Among the Five Civilized Tribes

International Standard Book Numbers
Paperbound: 978-0-7884-4473-9
Clothbound: 978-0-7884-7549-8

Table of Contents

In their memory,

Lydia Talkington, and Patrick Drennan

Acknowledgments

When working on a new project, I have to pause and note those persons who have inspired me to stay focused. Because of so many people and their impact on my life, I am extremely grateful. I am grateful for the many cases that have been brought to my attention by historian Art T. Burton, whose scholarship has kept me focused on the richness of Indian Territory history. Researchers such as Bennie McCrae have contributed continually to the growth of my knowledge of other parts of Western Frontier history. Dr. Tiya Miles's work has kept my eyes, on the complexities of the structures of Black Indian families, especially through her research on the Shoeboots from the Cherokee Nation.

The works of scholars such as Claudio Saunt, and the efforts of the "new" activists in the Freedman community, such as Prof. Carla Pratt, Attorney Demario Solomon Simmons, have brought about a new spirit of enthusiasm to myself and to others. The knowledge gleaned from the works of Daniel F. Littlefield, not only in terms of what he has written, but also the time and commitment that he is made is deeply appreciated. I appreciate the time that he has spent with me, and with others in this struggle to tell the stories yet untold.

Thanks also to a good friend Paula Ashby whose encouragement and friendship is constant, who always encourages me to tell Sam and Sallie's story. Genealogy colleague Argyrie McRay has been very helpful to me, for she always reminds me of the value of local county resources and has shared some of those treasures on numerous research ventures. Also appreciation goes to Agnes Kane Callum, the mentor to many of us, and who has been the example to follow, of how one has to recognize the need to tell one's story oneself.

Special thanks and appreciation are owed to dear friend, and colleague, Tonia Holleman. She continues to teach me the simple joys of discovery and research and whose friendship has added a new dimension to my work and projects. Her research skills with Choctaw, Chickasaw, and Creek Freedmen continue to inspire and encourage me to keep going. From the countless cemeteries we visited, to archives, and libraries, her presence has shown me the need to continually comb through the pages and this has taken me down new paths of discovery.

Special thanks also to Ronald Walton, who painstakingly assists in documenting burial sites, and whose meticulousness in record keeping is a reminder of the need to document accurately.

Fellow Freedman researcher Terry Ligon is also owed special thanks. It is he who has followed the legacy of his own Chickasaw ancestors from over a century ago. Through his discoveries, new stories have arisen and a new publication has emerged, and his tenacity and curiosity have taught me countless lessons.

Few projects are finished without the love and joys that come from family. I do thank my dear niece, Olivia, whose spirit always brings sunshine into my life. Also special thoughts and thanks to my god-daughter Angela, whose future reminds me of joys of looking ahead.

And finally I must thank my husband, Ganiyu Raji, whose love and support are constant, whose enthusiasm is genuine, and whose encouragement is continuous. Without his patience, and understanding, this book would not have been completed.

Introduction

Since the publication of the first edition of my book *Black Indian Genealogy Research*, I have had many opportunities to reflect upon the beginning of my own interest in family history in general and African-Native American genealogy in particular. The genealogical journey has been one that continues to point me towards new places from ancient burial grounds to long forgotten settlements and towns in what is now Oklahoma. More often than not, I still recall the wonderment that was instilled in my childhood mind, on family trips into eastern Oklahoma, and the directions that my imagination took when the small historical marker on Highway 64, greeted travelers as they headed into the old Cherokee Nation, into what was at one time, Indian Territory.

"Entering Indian Territory" These were the words that often caught my attention as our family drove westward from Ft. Smith Arkansas into eastern Oklahoma. Passing pecan groves along the Arkansas River and the unfolding fields of alfalfa was fascinating, but that historic marker would greet us less than 5 miles into the state, and my imagination would soar.

As a child growing up in the 1950s that sign always stimulated in my imagination scenes from the television westerns, that dominated the screen during those days. That sign would also seem to bring about my father's declaration of the Choctaw ancestry of our gr. grandmother Sallie Walton whom we affectionately called Nannie. Of course, how she connected to the television images of Indians never made sense to me, but somehow officially being in Indian country, which the historical marker declared, somehow added to the mystique of our having Indian blood and my child's imagination was fueled. I did wonder how such

1

delightful gentle brown woman who always made me some sassafras was actually connected to the images on television of Indians from the many television westerns. I never saw the connection at all, but the one thing I knew, was that something called "Indian Territory" was real, and that she was real, and that was all that mattered.

The remainder of the 2-hour ride that seemed endless, to visit my Aunt Pat and Uncle John in Oktaha, and the many cousins, I would sit in the back seat of the car with my brother. I watched closely scanning the countryside full of soy beans and alfalfa rolling by. I remember straining my eyes to see the Indians if we took a detour through Sallisaw, or Vian. I would stare in to the faces of the local townspeople, seeing tanned, brown, red, white and black faces wondering how many of them had Indian blood like we did. I would later learn that perhaps most of those white, black, and red faces were part of the Indians I had hoped to see.

Arrival at Aunt Pat's in the country town of Oktaha meant food—lots of country food, ham, chicken, and barbecue, and the chance to run around and feel the country life around me. I didn't realize that I was in the heart of the Creek Nation, and was less than two miles from the famous Honey Springs Battlefield--the most significant Civil War battlefield of Indian Territory. Only recently did I notice that the back of what was Uncle John's property there was a sign that pointed to that very site.

I was a listener as a child, and having been around elderly people, I had learned to listen well. The visit to Aunt Pat's would include talks among the elders about their youth. My fascination would return, and once again I would hear mention of Indians and places with exotic names--Checotah, Tullahasse, and Redbird and Rentiesville.

My school days were spent in the western Arkansas city of Ft. Smith. The city has a rich history of its own, much of it affiliated with Indian Territory. The Federal Western District Court was located there, with the infamous Judge Isaac C. Parker, the "Hanging Judge" holding court. But I would be an adult before I would ever learn of the rich legacy of the Black and Indian Deputy U.S. Marshals who rode for Judge Parker.

When at play, I often heard of the playmates boasting about their ties to the Oklahoma Indians. In most cases the reference was to the Cherokee Nation and many playmates would remark that there was a family connection to someone who was a chief in the Cherokee Nation. Interestingly, once the talk about ancestry would begin, others would join the verbal bravado. Most of us actually doubted than any of the stories were true. But then there were those who insisted----- over and over that they were a part of the Cherokee Nation and that they were really part Indian.

My gr. grandmother Sallie died in 1961. I was particularly close to her, and upon her death, when her Bible was passed to my father. I often found myself gingerly holding on to it, treasuring some lingering connection to her. Folded inside of that Bible was a plat map, with Sallie Walton's name on it, and the words "Choctaw Nation" stamped inside of it. The family history section of the Bible contained names of persons unknown to me–Lydia, Amanda and Houston. The names were clues to the family history, but they were not enough to tell me the entire story. Sallie's few pictures of herself and her brother revealed a mixed ancestry, but still there were no real pointers to the larger story of her life and history.

It would not be until 1991, some thirty years after Sallie's death that I would finally learn some facts about her life. Having relocated to Maryland, I had committed myself to taking full advantage of being able to use the records of the National Archives in Washington DC. I had been directed to look at the documents from Record Group 75, which contained items pertaining to the Five Civilized Tribes. I knew that Sallie was from the Choctaw Nation, and that the Choctaws were part of the Five Civilized Tribes.

I had always noticed a small piece of paper, half torn that had Sallie's name on it, and I knew it was significant, because it too, was kept in her Bible. On that paper was her name and a number behind it and a code of some sort, that simply said, "Choc. Fr." Not sure of what that meant, on that visit to the Archives in May of 1991, I learned that Choc. Fr. meant Choctaw Freedmen.

Exploring some microfilmed documents called *Enrollment Cards* I looked at the many names as they rolled by on the screen. One name did catch my eye—that of Joe Perry. Sallie had a brother by that name. We called him Uncle Joe, and he was the very fair-skinned elderly man who visited her. I was not sure if this card pertained to our Uncle Joe or not, but it did catch my attention, if nothing else. But I kept scrolling through dozens more names on the microfilm reader. When I got to the 700th Enrollment Card, and considered stopping, but decided to continue and decided that I would at least look at the first 1000 cards scrolling quickly before leaving the archives that day. Somehow, as if I had been driven there, the card number 777 made me stop. There they were! The Walton family! There were their names, Samuel Walton, Sallie Walton, Sam Walton Jr., Houston Walton and someone unknown to me, called Louisa. These were the names in the Bible----all but Louisa's– but both Samuels were there, and so was Houston,

4

and this was our family—the same names listed in Sallie's Bible. I was overtaken with excitement and emotion. I sat there staring at those names telling me that I had found my own family, my ancestors among the Choctaws.

The records that I had found that day on the Walton family of Choctaw Freedmen led me to a vast array of additional records. The names of *"new"* ancestors were gleaned form the first set of records, Lydia and Patrick, Eastman Williams Sallie's father, he was a previously unknown Choctaw Indian man, whose name I had never heard.

The discovery of the first set of Dawes records, the Enrollment cards led me down a new path of discovery, through unknown parts of Oklahoma history. A set of records called the Applications for Enrollment for the Five Civilized Tribes allowed me to read the actual words spoken by my ancestors, as they appeared in front of the Dawes Commission. In that interview they spoke of their lives as slaves and as free people.

My quest to learn more details about their lives in Indian Territory has taken me along an incredible journey as a genealogist as a researcher and as student of American history.

In the past 12 years, I have begun to read and more records of Indian Territory from those that pre-date the Civil War, to those that followed Oklahoma statehood. The most critical fact has emerged for me, that Oklahoma's history is very complicated, and it is as versatile as the history of the frontier itself.

The Dawes Records are only a tip of the iceberg, I have learned. There are military records of the Black Indians, both as U.S. Colored Troops and as Indian Home Guards. The records of the Loyal Creeks created right after the Civil War reflect the lifestyle of several hundred Africans in the Creek Nation. In contrast, the files from the Criminal Case Records of Ft. Smith reveal other tales of Black Indian lawmen, and Black Indian outlaws both of whom left paper trails to be researched. Tribal court records and even congressional records have now emerged to open doors for family historians and researchers.

I continue to locate new documents pertaining to the African-Native American people. Some records are organized and indexed while others are not. The years have pointed out to me, that the story is larger than a story of Oklahoma, and I have had to open my eyes to the records from the Southeastern United States as well. The records of the Eastern Cherokee and the Mississippi Choctaws are among the records that I have begun to study for more knowledge of the Black Indian story. All Indians did not relocate to the west, thus a rich Black Indian legacy thrives among those remaining people in the southeast as well.

As a result the past decade has been one of educating and re-educating myself. I shall, in this revised work expand upon the kinds of records available for research. I shall address the basic myths and realities of Black Indian genealogy. The focus of this work is therefore to discuss the basics of using the most available records, to discuss how to use sound genealogical research methods and to present various family cases where the family's story can be told on many levels.

Chapter 1

Researching Slavery in the Indian Nations Myths and Realitites

Chapter 1

Understanding Slavery in the Indian Nations. Myths and Realities

"But didn't their kind of slavery offer protection for the black people with whom they shared a common enemy? Didn't the Indian slave owners frequently adopt their slaves and treat them as brothers?"

These are questions that I often hear from persons who have heard for the first time that African chattel slavery existed in the Indian nations. Persons who have a basic assumption of a shared alliance between black slaves and American Indians to avoid a common oppressor make this assumption repeatedly.

The one thing that genealogy research does is to compel the researcher to face the realities of the historical context in which their ancestors lived. One of those realities for Black Indian researchers is that black chattel reality was a harsh reality for the slaves, and that it is from this "peculiar institution," from which there thousands of documents remain and from which hundreds of thousands of descendants can research their family history.

In order to begin to research for African ancestors among the Indians, it is important to have a full understanding of the origins of the contact between Africans and Native Americans. Since the institution of slavery brought the first Africans to America, it is critical to begin at that point in African American history. In addition, the arrival of the settlers to America coincided with the seizure of American land from its native people. These two events the arrival of settlers and the arrival of African slaves,

9

occurred simultaneously and contributed to the early contacts between blacks and Indians.

There is a common perception among many individuals that slaver in America consisted entirely of African people enslaved by whites. Yet there were many whites who were enslaved or indentured, many blacks who were free, and many Native Americans who owned black slaves. It is true that the great majority of the slaves in America were Africans, and the great majority of the slave owners were white. Likewise it is also important to learn that not all Native Americans had confrontational relationships with whites and that many embraced the institution of African slavery. This is something, which the black family historian should keep in mind when searching for ancestors.

In 1981, noted author J. Leitch Wright referred to the history of Black and Native American relations in his work, *The Only Land They Knew*. He mentioned in his work the observation made by historian Carter G. Woodson that the relations between Native Americans and African Americans can be considered "one of the longest unwritten chapters in the history of the United States. [1]

He notes that the presence of Black Indians was the result of two simultaneous events: the enslavement of African in America, and the seizure of land form the Indians.[2] Wright points out that much has been written about the seizure of Indian lands, broken treaties and confrontations as the settlers moved westward. Likewise the

---

[1] Wright, J. Leitch, *The Only Land They Knew. The Tragic Story of American Indians in the Old South*. New York: The Free Press 1981, p. 248

[2] Ibid

horrors of the slave trade over the Atlantic and the methods and practices of slavery in America has been well researched. Yet so little has been written about slavery among the nations of Indians specifically those known today as the Five Civilized Tribes. Ironically, it is among the records from these nations that most documentation exists.

There have been some isolated works that have appeared over the years. Annie Abel in the early part of the 20th century did address the history of American Indians in her pivotal work, *The American Indian as Slave Owner and Secessionist*[3].

Other works from the noted scholar Kenneth Wiggins Porter addressed Africans among the Seminoles as well as blacks who lived on the western frontier. Scholar Laurence Foster did look into the experiences of blacks before removal in his work *"Negro-Indian Relationships in the Southeast"* that also looked at relations with black people and Seminoles. Daniel F. Littlefield has vigorously researched the contact between black and native peoples in his many works on Indian Territory and the plight of the African Native people there.[4] The 1990's brought forth some new

---

[3] Abel, Annie Heloise *The American Indian as Slave holder and Secessionist*, Cleveland: Arthur H. Clark Company, 1915

[4] Littlefield's works should be collected and read by all with a strong interest in the Five Civilized Tribes. He cites cases, with strong documentation pertaining to the lives before and after relocation, and his works on Freedmen from the Cherokee and Chickasaw nations reflect the complicated plight of the Black Indians and their disenfranchisement from the nations where the were born, toiled and died. Freedmen descendants are particularly urged to read *The Cherokee Freedmen* and *The Chickasaw Freedmen* to gain a clearer understanding of the documents that they will utilize in their family history research efforts.

scholarship on the subject, and the work of Jack D. Forbes who looked at the culture and the language of race in his work *Africans and Native Americans.*[5]

It is known that indentured servitude, was introduced to America as early as 1619 in Jamestown Virginia and by the time of the America Revolution in the 1770s the practice of slavery had deeply entrenched itself in American culture. As more European settlers came to America more of the indigenous people were pushed away from their native land. Although most Indians resisted and resented the white settlers, there were other who were less hostile to the invaders and learned some of the their cultural practices. The Native Americans in the Southeastern United States had the earliest exposures to the Europeans. Their contact these foreigners were not always violent, and in time they were associating with traders, missionaries and government representatives. As a result, many of the natives embraced the religion of the newcomers and adopted European traders and architecture.

Noted historian Angie Debo who wrote extensively about the Five Civilized Tribes, points out that the first two hundred and fifty years of contact with whites brought few changes in their fundamental social institutions. But by the 19th century, after decades of trading, the Tribes had acquired the implements and weapons of Western Europe. From 1800 on, the Indians of the Southeast sought to adopt the ways of the settlers, with a constitutional government, the Christian religion and the institution of African slavery. In the process, they made the transition from the old Indian culture in which they had been primarily hunters and gatherers to a new Indian culture in which they were primarily Southern

---

[5] Forbes, Jack, <u>Africans and Native American Americans. The Lanugage or Race and the Evolutin of Red-Black Peoples.</u> Urbana and Chicago: University of Illinois press 1993

farmers. This transition to an agrarian culture brought about the purchase of large tracts of land by the Indians. And like their European neighbors, they found that large farms required workers to tend to the land. As a result, African slavery became economically valuable to the Indians, just as it had to the rest of the south. The adaptation to European ways occurred mainly among the Cherokees, Choctaw, Chickasaw, Creeks and the Seminoles, who thus became known as the "Five Civilized Tribes."

The purchase and ownership of black slaves by the Indians cannot be ignored. Once the family researcher understands this, the information may lead many African American families to detailed records pertaining to their ancestors. These records will be found among the Indian Freedmen records of the Five Civilized Tribes.

Initially, it is essential that the researcher confront some of the myths about the black-Indian relations. Among those myths are the assumptions that black could consider Indians as allies most of the time, and that Indians would embrace them as runaways into their communities. It is true that there were many instances where Indians and blacks were comrades, but the institution of slavery among the Five Tribes altered that situation. Once slavery instilled itself, a source of potential allies immediately dried up for blacks that might attempt to flee bondage.[6] Later, in the 19th century many blacks from other states would be recognized as Indian fighters including the famous Buffalo Soldiers of Southwest. The slaves from Indian Territory were not Buffalo soldiers,

---

[6] Like the slave rebellions of Nat Turner in Virginia and Denmark Vesey in South Carolina, Indian Territory also had its slave rebellion. The 1842 Slave Rebellion influenced the Cherokees, to establish harsh slave codes when the slaves of Joseph Vann rebelled, and initiated what the Cherokees called the *Great Runaway*. This instilled even more harsh laws pertaining to movement of slaves within the tribes.

but the assumed natural alliance between the races, was not uniformly there, either.

By the end of the 18th century slavery was solidly planted in the southeast United States and just as solidly into the life an culture of the five largest tribes. Dr. R. Halliburon Jr, in his work *"Red Over Black. Black Slavery Among the Cherokee Indians,"* points out that when on is evaluating the incidence of slavery among the Indians, one should not make assumptions about the nature of the slavery practiced among these tribes. He notes that there are perceptions that are inaccurate among Indians and among non-Indians, such as the belief that Indians were "kinder" slave masters. Each nation handled slavery differently, just as each nation had its own special relations with white settlers.[7]

Halliburton notes that by the late 1700's the Cherokees began intermarrying with whites, and the mixed blood Indians (Indian and white) became and remained the principle slave owners. These mixed bloods also emerged as the wealthiest of the Indians. With the increase of slaves, Halliburton also points out another significant fact: despite the steady increase in the number of slaves, there were never any abolition societies to emerge in any of the Five Civilized Tribes, not any expressions of discontent with the institution of slavery from the tribes. As a result slavery became an accepted fact of life especially for wealthy Indians.[8] Slaves were a convenient and inexpensive way to profit from the farms, which became a part of their lifestyle. The new chiefs emerged from the mixed blood slave owners, and many had massed a great amount of wealth by the early 1800s.

---

[7] Halliburton, R. Jr. <u>Red Over Black. Black Slavery Among the Cherokee Indians</u> Westport Connecticut: Greenwood Press. 1977 p. 4

[8] Ibid, p. 5

The Cherokees

It is known that Nancy Ward was one of the first women in the Cherokee nation to own black slaves. In 1755, when her husband was killed, she obtained his weapon and became a warrior herself in the Battle of Taliwa against the Creeks. Her people were the victors in that battle and she received a captured black slave as a prize.[9] Within a few short years, Nancy Ward became the owner of several slaves, purchasing many of her own. By the end of the1790s the Cherokees began to lose a great amount of land to the whites and being unhappy, they began to also raid villages and settlements of squatters. Halliburton points out that frequently in such encounters, whites were killed and blacks were frequently taken as prisoners. Likewise, other Cherokees began actually purchasing black slaves of their won on a regular basis.

John Ross, originally from Tennessee was an important Cherokee Chief who was wealthy and who was a major slave owner. Before removal to Oklahoma his slaves worked five major fields of his estate. John Martin, another tribal leader owned well over 100 slaves. The Vanns were equally as wealthy and were a part of the landed gentry class of Cherokee slave owners. This wealth transcended removal, and after the forced relocation of the Cherokees on the well documented *"Trail of Tears"* the presence of African slaves on that removal is never mentioned, but the slaves survived

---

[9] The story of Nancy Ward's bravery states that her husband was first engaged in battle, and he received a fatal blow from the enemy. Enraged at her husband's death, she ran to his side, seized his weapon, and attacked his assassin. Such a demonstration of bravery, courage and strength was not seen often in battle from a woman, therefore, she was given the highest honor the nation bestowed upon women. She was then referred to as *Ghighau,* or "most beloved woman."

relocation to support the wealthy landowner lifestyle of the leaders.

By 1809 the Cherokee nation began to enact laws by the National council and in 1827 the Cherokee nation adopted a constitution patterned after that of the United States. It is interesting to note some of the passages pertaining to slavery.

> ***Article III, Section 4: No person shall be eligible to a seat in the General Council but a free Cherokee male citizen, who shall have attained to the age of twenty-five years. The descendants of Cherokee men by all free women, except the African race, whose parents may have been living together as man and wife, according to the customs and laws of this Nation, shall be entitled to all the rights and privileges of the Nation, as well as the posterity of Cherokee women by all free men. No person who is of Negro or Mulatto parentage either by the father or mother's side, shall be eligible to hold any office or profit, honor or trust under this Government.*** [10]

In addition, it is significant to understand that not only in the Southeast, but also in many parts of Indian country, many native people were often encouraged to capture runaway slaves, for monetary rewards. In some instances free blacks were captured and held in bondage by Indians. An example is the case of Paul Smith. Smith had been manumitted in the early 1800s and he, being literate wrote a letter appealing to government authorities to secure his release from bondage, having been captured by Chief Doublehead.

---

[10] *Laws of the Cherokee Nation: Adopted by the Council at Various Periods* Tahlequah, Cherokee Nation: Cherokee Advocate Office 1852, p. 242-243

"My color unfortunately incapacitates me from applying personally to your honor. In 1802 my former master W. Smith, on his death ordered me to be liberated from bondage, by paying his son $400, the greater part of which I paid and was then liberated, Doublehead seized my property with myself, the cattle he retained for his own use, myself, he sold to Capt. John Campbell of the 2nd U.S. Regiment Infantry to the value of $400. I trust your honor will be so good as to interfere in my cause and obtain my freedom."[11]

For any researcher of Cherokee history, the most essential event to alter the destiny of the tribe resulted from the Indian Removal Act. This began the mass deportation of thousands of people from their homelands in the southeast United States to the lands in Arkansas and what is now Oklahoma. This forced exodus of red and black men and women to the new "Indian Territory" began in mid winter of 1830 with the Choctaws. By the end of that decade most of the other nations had been removed to the west.

For the Cherokees, the removal was particularly devastating. This was a physically painful march in which many lost their lives, and which is now historically referred to as the "Trail of Tears." However, it should be pointed out that among the Cherokees who began the march were 1600 black Cherokee slaves, who were pushed westward along with their masters. By 1840, thousands of Indians with their black slaves had been removed to the new Indian Territory.

In the testimonies of the freedmen later in this book there are some references to the "old country". This old

---

[11] Secretary of War Files, Indian Division No. 1484 National Archives, Paul Smith to Henry Dearborn

country was of course, the original homeland of the Indians east of the Mississippi.

The Slave Rebellion

The year 1842 was to bring about the strictest controls upon slaves in the Cherokee nation. This was because during the spring of that year, about the major slave uprising in Indian Territory occurred. Approximately 200 slaves, mostly Cherokee, though it is said that some Creek slaves joined the rebellion, escaped from the estate of Joseph *"Rich Joe"* Vann in Webbers Falls. In the early hours of that spring morning, the homes of the slave owners were locked, while the horses, mules gun and other weapons were seized along with food and supplies, and the slaves fled.

The intention was to reach Mexico, a land that many had heard was a land where slavery did not legally exist. After obtaining a fresh supply of horses and supplies from Ft. Smith, the slave owners eventually caught up with the slaves, and after an engaging battle, the slaves ran out of food, ammunition, and most importantly, water, and were forced to surrender. The leaders were executed, and many of the males were confined to work on Joseph Vann's boats for the remainder of their lives.

The slave rebellion, immediately had its consequences throughout the nation. There had been some free blacks who had lived in the nation peacefully among the Cherokees, and immediately restrictions were put upon them. In December, the national council passed legislation to remove free blacks from the nation.

Sec. 1, Be it enacted by the national council That it be made the duty of the sheriffs of the several districts of this nation to notify all free Negroes who may be in this nation, excepting such as have been

18

freed by our citizens, that they must leave the limits of this nation by the first day of January 1843 or as soon thereafter as may be practical.

Sec. 2 Be it further enacted, That should any free Negroes, as aforesaid, refuse to obey the order of the sheriffs, it shall be the duty of such sheriffs to report such Negro or Negroes to the United States agent for the Cherokees for immediate expulsion from this nation.[12]

The Creeks, Chickasaws and Choctaws

The first use of the term "civilized tribe" comes form a reference to the Creeks. They were accustomed to trade and they were known to have interacted with the whites early on. The creeks frequently traveled from Georgia and Alabama to trade furs in Pensacola, Florida. As a result it was not unusual for Creek women to marry white traders. Actually this was how European surnames became a part of most of the indigenous tribes. As the Indian women married European men, names such as Ross, McIntosh, Love, LeFlore, Johnson were not unusual in Indian communities.

In addition to marriages, many Indian men and women adopted European style of dress and weaponry. Because they embraced the settlers' ways so well they were considered a "civilized" tribe.

By 1800, wealthy Choctaws began purchasing large number of black slaves and for thousands of African slaves in this region possible escape routes vanished as slavery found itself practiced in the Indian nations. By the 19th

---

[12] Halliburton, p. 87

19

century, race became a critical factor for these Indians in judging people, whereas race as a concept was not a part of the way of life prior to that time. Slave codes were adopted and laws were enacted among the Indians to control the slaves, to prevent intermarriage and to prevent the slaves from becoming literate. Runaways were often reported in Indian newspapers as well. In the *Choctaw Intelligencer*, a bilingual newspaper published in Indian Territory in the 1850s one can find many ads pertaining to runaway slaves offering rewards for their capture, and there were often other articles pertaining to the value of slavery to the tribe.

The Creeks were also unique in their history, because they had a good number of free persons of color, free Africans who lived among them. In any number of texts, one will find maps and references to Africans, who lived before and after removal among mostly the Lower Creeks, After removal to the Territory, persons such as Cow Tom, Harry Island, and Silas Jefferson would emerge as critical leaders among the Muskogee Creeks. In other texts one can find even maps where free blacks lived, and in the years after the civil war, a majority of the black towns of Indian Territory, would be right in the very heart of that nation.

Life in the Territory

Once those who survived the removal to the west had arrived, two distinct social classes emerged among many of the Indians. The slave owners formed the aristocracy. They were most often mixed bloods and were the more prosperous. The rest of the people were full bloods who owned fewer slaves, and who had little power in their respective nations. Not surprisingly, what resulted was a way of thinking in which a proportion of white blood was considered more positive, pure Indian blood a little less positive, and a proportion of black blood was considered to be the most negative trait. This concept would carry itself into the issues that emerged, decades later when the Dawes Commission would determine how much land would be given to various persons. In some tribes, those with African blood, designated as *Freedmen* received the least amount of land among those who were allotted land.

It is assumed by many who first learn of the enslavement of black people by Indians that the slavery practiced by the Indians was not as harsh as slavery practiced by whites. However, in spite of this, many slaves still attempted to escape from their enslavers. The dramatic attempt of the Cherokees in the revolt of the 1842 had its affect in other nations such as the Creek and Seminole nations, since both nations had free blacks living among them. The Choctaw and Chickasaw nations did not have black towns and settlements.

If one looks for places in Indian Territory where the lives of slaves resembled the lives of black slaves in the deep south, the Choctaw and Chickasaw nations both would be the places. However, on the other hand, the slaves within those nations, lived within the cultural context of the nations, and would later still practice burial customs, dietary customs and in many cases, would be a bilingual people, before and after Oklahoma statehood.

There were other attempts at revolts that would occasionally arise in Indian Territory, most of which would be met with early defeats. From the 1840s, until the beginning of the Civil War, unrest was reported from "outlaw Negroes" particularly along the Choctaw/Cherokee border.

The Black Seminoles

It is very important to distinguish the history of the Seminoles form the other tribes, especially for the family historian. Unlike the other four nations, the Seminoles truly differed in their perception of slavery from the Europeans and those who are looking for ancestors black or red, in the Seminole Nation will find both sets of Seminole records - Seminoles by Blood and Seminole Freedmen useful in their research. Many of the application records in the Seminole Freedmen, section are missing because blood transferred some freedmen to the regular rolls of Seminoles.

Like the other nations in the southeast, the Seminoles had early exposure to whites. Likewise, these Indians adopted some European customs. Their culture grew out of the Creeks and so the similarity must be noted. In addition, by the early 1800s there were some blacks living in some of the Seminole settlements in northern Florida. At first these Indians welcomed the blacks in their lands and the blacks that settled there eventually adopted an Indian way of life. Although they lived in separate villages, many of the customs of these blacks as well as their spoken language was the Muskogee of the Seminoles. A typical Seminole village contained both freedmen as well as slaves. It has been estimated that at one time there were 1400 black Seminoles, with only 200 of those blacks believed to be slaves of the Indians.[13]

With the Cherokees, their major disagreement with the whites was over land, but with the Seminoles, their friction with whites was the nature of their form of slavery. [14] It is often stated that in the Seminole nation black slaves

---

[13] Littlefield, Daniel F. *African and Seminoles,* Westport, Connecticut: Greenwood Press, p. 12.

had arms, grew their own food and had more freedom of movement. The southern white slaves owners feared that these black villages of Northern Florida would be too great at temptation to their own slaves who might see Florida as a place of refuge. A good number of the conflicts of the Second Seminole War occurred when the U.S. Army strove to destroy the Seminole villages and to move in white settlers who had a different concept of slavery.

The Seminoles both black and full bloods fought intensely for their rights to remain in Florida. The black Seminoles had more to lose than simply land, since their defeat meant the inevitable return to the more severe form of slavery practiced by the whites, and by the other Indian nations. The resistance in Florida of black Seminoles occurred when John Horse surrendered in 1838, however, it should be noted that this Black Seminole leader would later emerge in the New Territory, as a strong leader, who would later take a large following into Mexico, successfully.

It should be noted that the records that were created when the Seminoles were removed to the west, provide some valuable documents for family historians. Many families of prominent black Seminoles, such as the family of Negro Abraham, as well as countless numbers of manumissions, were provided to insure the safe transport of records of these African Seminoles to Indian Territory. The 1860 Federal Census of "Lands West of Arkansas" contains the names of some of the Seminoles who had come to Indian Territory as free people. The largest family is that of Abraham. The family is enumerated in the 1860 census as the family of Abraham Payne.

---

[14] Ibid

Life in Indian Territory was not without its challenges, even for the Black Seminoles. They had been given the promise of living as free people in the territory. But upon their arrival at Fort Gibson, slave agents were waiting for them. The Creeks, who were old enemies of the Seminoles kidnapped many of the Black Seminoles and sold them within their own nation. In regard to other blacks it was declared that whoever was a slave before the Second Seminole War, was to remain a slave after arriving in Indian Territory. About 300 slaves were immediately returned to the Seminole "masters" who bought them back. Many of these black Seminoles eventually settled in the village of Wewoka under John Horse, their leader from the old nation in Florida.

Because the spirit of the Seminole blacks was still very strong, there were constant attacks upon them by slave hunters, some from the Creek Nation. Many of these blacks felt that an escape from Indian Territory was the only answer to their situation. In 1849, only seven years after the Cherokee Slave revolt, a sizeable group of black Seminoles left Indian Territory together with some full blood Seminoles. By the summer of 1850, these men and women arrived at the Mexican border. One large contingent of them was successful in crossing the border and subsequently settled in northern Mexico. This escape to freedom is significant because in spite of the comparative freedom they had, there was still that instinctive human desire to be truly free and in charge of one's own life. One of the most detailed and poignant descriptions of the exodus from Indian Territory into Mexico can be found in the work of Kenneth Wiggins Porter. He describes how Wild Cat and John Horse had endured many assaults upon their freedom in Indian Territory.

According to Wiggins, John Horse defied the orders of the U.S. government to remain at Ft. Gibson, and had moved a band of Seminoles and Black Seminoles to Wewoka Creek. He and his band of followers cleared much of the land and made efforts to establish a settlement there and to begin their lives as free people. However, attacks continued, from predatory slave hunters as well as from some of the Creeks to also enslave them. The exodus began not in one large group, but in several bands of Seminole Indians and blacks that traveled, with much difficulty through Texas, encountering hostile attacks from the Comanches and others. At times other Indians joined some of the bands of Seminoles, both black and red, on their trek southwards.[15] This relocation occurred from 1849-1850.

The concept of race had changed dramatically among the nations known as the Five Civilized Tribes. The early days of contact when Spanish sailors arrived in the Americas with blacks as sailors, and later as slaves, and the beginnings of the African slave trade brought about a new acculturation in each of the five tribes. As time passed, the relationships even with free blacks would also be affected. In some cases free blacks lived among the nations in the Territory and settled freely such as with the Creeks, who at the same time, owned a good number of slaves. It would not be until the abolishment of slavery in Indian Territory that a larger adoption of blacks would occur formally in the nation. The Seminoles, who had assimilated the least with whites, had no rigorous slave codes as the other nations. They adopted blacks immediately after the Civil War, and in many situations, the blacks had lived in a state that would not in many cases even be described as enslavement. The Chickasaws were, in contrast very unyielding in terms of citizenship and embracing their former slaves, and fought for decades against adoption of their slaves. They were

---

[15] Porter, Kenneth W. The Black Seminoles. History of a Freedom Seeking People, Gainsville Florida: University Press of Florida, 1996. p. 128-130

successful in their efforts, as they never adopted the Freedmen. The Choctaws adopted the Freedmen in 1885, and the Creek and Cherokees had adopted their former slaves immediately.

Interestingly, the Creek nation had a closer relationship socially before and after the Civil War, and made many provisions to insure the rights of their African citizens.[16] The African Creeks contributed to the political life of the Creek Nation and for the four decades that followed the Civil War, up until Oklahoma statehood, dynamic black Creek leaders would influence the politics of the nation. From the records of the Freedmen leaders, rich history is found, and for Creek researchers, it will be critical to also follow the documents pertaining to these leaders. The famed Dawes records of the Creek nation, are believed to have been hidden, and therefore were not microfilmed, so there is a gap in one set of records. However, when one studies the lives of several of the Freedman leaders, such as Silas Jefferson, Sugar George, Scipio Sango, Monday Durant, Cow Tom and Harry Island, and Pickett Rentie, much rich history of African Creek families can be gleaned. In addition, many of the families inter-married, so hundreds of descendants of these families will be able to still document rich history from the records that did survive.

---

[16] Littlefield, Daniel F. Jr. *Africans and Creeks. From the Colonial Period to the Civil War* Westport, Connecticut:1979 p. 259

Chapter 2

From Slavery to Freedom

Chapter 2

From Slavery To Freedom

*"As natives we are attached to the people among whom we
have been born and bred. We like the Chickasaws as
friends and we know by the experience of the past that we
can live with them in a close union."*

Memorial of the Chickasaw Freedmen

By the time the Civil War arrived, Indian Territory
was bordered on the east by Arkansas, which had become
one of the states having seceded from the Union. It was not
long be-fore the Five Civilized Tribes each had signed
treaties forming an alliance with the Confederate States. The
Chickasaws and Choctaws were the first to form an alliance
with the southern states, although considerable divisions
occurred among both nations before they officially formed
this alliance.

There were some contingents of Indians who wanted
to live out the war in peace and to not involve themselves in
the confrontations. With the Creeks, one of the stronger
bands was centered around the leadership of a wealthy Creek
Chief, Opothole Yahola. His primary motivation was to stay
out of the Civil War, not to sympathize with either side.
However, he eventually armed himself and led a group of red
and black men into the northern part of Indian Territory, and
they actually held a significant stronghold for a while. But
the sentiments of the other nations were with the
Confederacy and Opothole Yahola and his followers
eventually left for Kansas, and then joined the forces
fighting, with the Union army.

A good number of blacks joined the Kansas Colored
Infantry, and many would have the opportunity to return to

the Territory in the famous Battle of Honey Springs. It was in this particular battle that some of the Indian fighters sympathetic to the South would encounter some of their former slaves as Union soldiers and would actually suffer defeat by these black soldiers.

It will be from the records that emerged from Opothole Yahola's movement into Kansas that some of the first "rolls" of Black Indians, particularly the Black Creeks will be found, as they enlisted in the military. Yahola's movement into Kansas would lead directly to the formation of several regiments of soldiers, the First Second and Third Indian Home Guards. It is from some of the regimental muster rolls of these regiments that Africans, both free and enslaved would be enlisted.

At the same time, in Kansas the state was also forming regiments of all escaped Blacks from Missouri, Northwest Arkansas as well as Indian Territory. They formed, the First and Second Kansas Colored Infantries and dozens were part of the same group of Black Creeks and Cherokees who made the great exodus into Kansas. The Kansas Colored infantries would later be re-designated as United States Colored Troops, forming the 79th and 83rd Infantries of the United States Colored troops. All of these regiments would become major players in Civil War battles in Indian Territory.[1]

---

[1] *The Battle of Honey Springs would become historic in that white, red and black soldiers would fight on the same side in the Union Army. Their combined efforts prevented Confederate forces from encroaching upon and seizing Ft. Gibson. The Union victory is actually attributed to the 1st Kansas Colored consisting of free and enslaved Black Cherokees, Creeks and some slaves also from Arkansas and Missouri in the regiments.*

The genealogical significance of this military information cannot be overlooked. The pension files of the soldiers from the Home Guards, the United States Colored Troops and the Kansas Colored, will reveal critical family data that cannot be overlooked, particularly regarding the unique history of the Africans of Indian Territory. In addition, the muster rolls, often reflect the bilingual and bicultural nature of the blacks from Indian nations. Their Indian names often appear next to a more anglicized name, followed usually by references to their physical features from copper to red, to black. Many of the soldiers in the Home Guards, enlisted with their traditional Creek names, but a quick glance at how their features were described gives evidence to the strong participation of African Creeks, in this effort.

Although the muster rolls, created for the purpose of military enlistment, researchers are encouraged to become familiar with them, particularly because they were not created for political manipulations within any tribe. They are significant because they reflect the actual bi-cultural status under which these individuals lived. These same individuals would later be designated simply as *"Freedmen"*.

As all genealogists who research the records of enslaved people know, it is critical to research the history of the slave owners as well as the history of the enslaved, to learn more about the story of one's family. Therefore, the records that reveal details about the Indian enslavers will be equally as essential in the quest to learn more of the family history. As a result, the knowledge of the records of the Confederate Indians is also essential when studying the history of the Civil War in Indian Territory. The following Confederate units came from the various Indian Territory nations: The 1st Cherokee Mounted Rifles, the 1st Chickasaw Infantry, the 1st Choctaw and Chickasaw Mounted Rifles, the

1st Creek Mounted Volunteers, the 2nd Cherokee Mounted Volunteers and the 2nd Creek Mounted Volunteers. There were smaller divisions within these units and a complete listing of these can be obtained in the Microfilm Guide to American Indians, published by the National Archives.[2]

The defeat of the Confederacy brought a new price for the Indians to pay. Since they had aligned themselves with the Confederacy, all previous treaties between the tribes and the United States were broken. In addition, a significant portion of land assigned to the Five Civilized Tribes was given to the Plains Nations, particularly the Shawnee and Delaware. Like their fellow slave owners in the South, they were now ordered to free all of their slaves, and to give these *freedmen,* as they were now so-called, equality in the Territory and in their tribes. Most slaves were freed in the United States in 1865, with the 13th Amendment to the U.S. Constitution, however the emancipation of the slaves in Indian Territory was not official until all of the Emancipation treaties were signed in 1866, in Ft. Smith, Arkansas.

In retaliation for their alliances with the South, the United States chose to "punish" the nations by seizing their land. However, a small number of about 1100 Creek citizens were identified as "Loyal Creeks" and were given some compensation for property lost during the war. Among this small group, were about 300 persons who had African Creek ancestry. Of those 300 approximately 60 soldiers from the Indian Home Guards were also identified.[3]

---

[2] National Archives Trust Fund. National Archives and Records Administration <u>American Indians. A Select Catalog</u>

[3] Sugar George, Harry Island, Monday Durant, all prominent in Creek Nation history, were among the black soldiers listed. These men were leaders in the Creek Nation till the turn of the century.

The significance of this roll of Loyal Creek claimants lies in the fact that some of the *"freedmen" who* were actually identified as having been slaves, lived with remarkable freedom, having owned property, and livestock. As a result of these claims, they did receive compensation. The claims reveal remarkable aspects about their lives in the mid 19th century and provide a real glimpse into their homes and towns before patrolling soldiers raided them, during the conflicts of war.

Researching the Lives of the Indian "Freedmen"

It is important to note that particularly in the Creek, Cherokee and Seminoles nations, that there were Africans who lived as both free persons and as enslaved persons. This does provide some opportunities for the genealogist to pursue.

Most freed blacks remained in Indian Territory, and most remained in the nation in which they had lived, whether as slaves or as free people. In the decades that followed, the freedmen established lives for themselves and made economic gains for themselves faster than the freedmen in the United States. Within the nations, there was some difficulty for the freedmen of the Choctaws and Chickasaws, especially if they had fought for the Union in the Civil War. Yet still, very few left the nations. Because they remained in the Territory, extensive documentation remains today, and one is able to get a glimpse of their lives in the mid 19th century western frontier.

Almost immediately after the war, came the desire to officially establish schools. The tradition of education was already strong in Indian Territory, with traditional academies already having been established. The Freedmen had the same thirst for education and the push for neighborhood schools came quickly. The Creek Freedmen were among the first to establish schools for freedmen, and within a short period of time Choctaw Colored Neighborhood schools arose, as did boarding academies. Tushka Lusa, a Choctaw name meaning *black warrior* was among the man neighborhood schools for the Choctaw Freedmen

By the turn of the century, the Tullahasse Freedmen School would become a gem in the Creek Nation, to be complemented by the beautiful grounds of Oak Hill Academy in the southeast Choctaw Nation. These schools would eventually die when Oklahoma statehood brought about a new system of segregated schools.

Not surprisingly, the thirst for learning could have been influenced by the fact that there was a high level of literacy in the Territory, and many of the former soldiers, were literate and they personally signed many of their statements when applying for their military pensions after the war. Efforts to establish rights for themselves became a major effort of the freedmen in the territory and some gains were made to receive money, land and schools. The major exception may be for those Chickasaw Freedmen who were given fewer privileges for almost four decades.[4]

1860 Federal Census

There were not many citizens of Indian Territory captured in the 1860 Federal Census. However, there is a small political jurisdiction that was captured nevertheless. It is a census of the "Free persons" who lived in the "Indian Lands West of Arkansas" as they were called. There were approximately 400 black people who were enumerated in Indian Territory in the various nations. Within the Seminole

---

[4] Littlefield, Daniel *The Chickasaw Freedmen. A People Without a Country* Westport, Conn.: Greenwood Press 1977 p 227

Nation, one can even locate the then aging but famed "Negro Abraham"[5] listed with his family. Many of the blacks enumerated were actually the bands that were followers of John Caesar and Abraham, and one will find Florida, and Georgia listed as the birthplace of many of these free people. The listing of the free blacks of 1860 census appears in the appendix. These free people cannot be viewed as having been slaves as their free status had been documented well.

In the Choctaw and Chickasaw nations the numbers of free blacks was fewer, however, this should not imply that the Choctaws or Chickasaws of African ancestry were any less bilingual, or bi-cultural than those in their neighboring nations of the Territory. In other publications and texts on Indian Territory history there are occasionally some maps that reflect the settlements of "free Negroes" in the years before the Civil War.

As the Civil War ended, the eventual signing of the Treaty of 1866 brought the beginning of even more rapid changes in the Territory. Slaves were now freed, more land was seized and now smaller than before and issues with other neighboring tribes would emerge, in addition to the invasion of other white settlers from the east, planning to move westward after the war.

Not surprisingly, the Seminoles were the first to welcome emancipation since they had many friends and family members among the enslaved population. They also immediately elected six freedmen to the 42-seat Seminole Council. Going back to the days before removal the Seminole Indians arrived Indian Territory as a nation of mixed people stemming from a more than 100 year

---

[5]   Abraham and his family are listed as the Payne family, and he and many of his neighbors reflect Florida as their birthplace.

relationship with Africans who had been fleeing from bondage in Georgia and Carolinas. The Seminole Wars had been fought primarily with the issue of returning runaway slaves into bondage. It would not be until the black Seminoles would be guaranteed status as free people and could emigrate to the Territory, that they finally agreed to leave as a group–both red and black together.

The Cherokees, Choctaws Chickasaws and Creeks eventually followed suit, but it took at least four decades of legal challenges to win land, education and citizenship for the former slaves of these nations. Note that in the 1840s a small group of several hundred Seminoles moved to Texas and Mexico. Some returned to the Territory after the war, but many were not allowed to become a part of the nation, and thus returned to the small settlement along the Texas Mexican border. Those remaining in Texas eventually were among those who were hired by the United States as scouts along the border.[6]

Angie Debo, in her book *The Rise and Fall of the Choctaw Republic* describes the Choctaw nation after the Civil War as a nation divided into three societies—the whites, the Indians and the Freedmen, that rarely mingled. In the Choctaw nation the schools were separate. However there was an informal mingling of the races with restrictions. When the various nation adopted their freedmen into the tribe as citizens, laws were immediately passed that made intermarriage felonies in their court systems.

However as strong as the sentiment was against inter-marriage, note that marriages did exist. The most interesting example of the complexities of life in Indian Territory

---

[6] Scott Thybony, "Against All Odds," *Smithsonian*, August 1994.

occurred within the structure of the Shoeboot family. This was an African Cherokee family, that survived post civil war restrictions against social norms, and carried their mixed legacy into the 20th century. The family stemmed from a former Confederate Cherokee soldier, Morrison Shoeboot who raised a family with his wife and former slave Dolly. Michigan professor Dr. Tiya Miles wrote her doctoral dissertation on the complexities of life that faced this mixed Black Cherokee family in 19th century post Civil War Indian Territory.[7]

Debo, in her work makes interesting references in her work to a secret society not unlike the Ku Klux Klan, that had one goal as its mission, in the Choctaw Nation, whose goal was to patrol the towns terrorizing Choctaw Freedmen right after the war. Because of the actions of this Vigilance Committee as it was called, a special commissioner to Indian Territory was appointed to guard the interests of the Freedmen. In addition, many of the Choctaw Freedmen often used the services of the Field office of the Freedmen's Bureau in nearby Ft. Smith, Arkansas.[8]

By the mid 1880s life was changing rapidly. Dozens of schools now dotted the town and settlements throughout the nations. The Choctaws, once reluctant to changes had made appropriations for their colored schools and by the 1890s thirty four colored neighborhood schools had been established. The Chickasaws had twenty one schools. The

---

[7] Miles, Tiya, <u>Ties That Bind: The Story of an Afro-Cherokee family in slavery and Freedom (American Crossroads)</u> Berkeley: University of California Press 2005

[8] The Freedmen's Bureau is known officially as the Office of Refugees, Freedmen and Abandoned Lands. Ft. Smith was one of the larger Field Offices and served not only western Arkansas, but also Indian Territory to assist Freedmen with their many problems after the war's end

nations continued in their tribal systems to debate and argue about the status of the freedmen, although in some of the same nations, freedmen had emerged as community leaders, town kings as in the Creek Nations. At the same time, while there was growing disenfranchisement developing, there was no mass exodus from the Territory. In the mid 1880s, the Chickasaws met and released a statement regarding their loyalty to the nations.

> *"As natives we are attached to the people among whom we have been born and bred. We like the Chickasaws as friends and we know by the experience of the past that we can live with them in a close union."*

This act of proving their presence in the territory in their respective nations would become the critical element for thousands of Blacks as they applied for enrollment in the five nations. Because of steady flow of free blacks and whites into Indian Territory after the War, the nations also had to now struggle to control this immigration into their land. Ironically even their statement of loyalty to the Chickasaw nation, the Chickasaw freedmen, were never adopted by the Chickasaw Nation.

In the late 1880s a land boom, mushroomed and the new settlers were determined to make the Territory their own state a new state of Oklahoma. The Creeks and Seminoles were forced to surrender their land right in Indian Territory and while this happened, the 1889 Land Rush was organized. One hundred thousand men, women and children entered the territory. It is estimated that about ten thousand of these immigrants were blacks from the Deep South.

Within a year, Indian Territory became a U.S. Territory, and by the 1890s there were 27 all black towns in what would eventually become Oklahoma. These towns consisted of both Indian freedmen and former United States slaves. During the same time, Edwin McCabe, a black Kansas state auditor launched plans to establish Oklahoma as a black state. However, both the Indian and white populations fought vigorously against that plan.

Within the Indian nations since statehood was becoming inevitable, final settlements were being made for all of the citizens of each nation. The "Black Indians" sought to be entered on the tribal rolls and to obtain the benefits of payment and land allotments being given to the other Indian citizens. When it was time to apply for enrollment, the Freedmen had to distinguish themselves from other blacks that had poured into the Territory after Emancipation, or during the Land Rush. The Commission established to make the political divisions to allot land to the citizens of the nation, and to eventually bring about the dissolution of the sovereignty of the nations was the infamous Dawes Commission.

Hundreds, of thousands of documents emerge from the works of the commission. The Freedmen records number also in the thousands and will be discussed in full detail. The Dawes Records provide much of the substance of the research of descendants of Indian Territory Freedmen, however, they are not the exclusive set of records upon which a researcher should rely. Like the census records, the Dawes Records were created for a political purpose, and there will be other bodies of records that will provide more clarity for researchers and that cannot be overlooked.

Eventually in Indian Territory each of the nations admitted their African citizens to some degree. However, with the Chickasaws, there was no official adoption, although the Freedmen were admitted and *"enrolled"* by the Dawes Commission. But their rights remained limited. The purpose of this process was for land and not for official citizenship.

Much activity arose when a major legal suit came from Bettie Ligon, a daughter of a major Chickasaw leader and a slave, when she sought enrollment and rights for her family and descendants to obtain tribal rights as citizens by blood. This legal battle would eventually bring in hundreds of persons connected to Bettie Ligon and the records of this case alone can also lead to a new genealogical avenue to follow.

It is from many sources, the tribal rolls, payment rolls, property claims, census records, and the thousands of Dawes Commission records from which the descendants of the Cherokees, Choctaws, Chickasaws, Creeks and Seminoles can begin research for their ancestors.

Chapter 3

Beginning Your Research With Indian Records

Chapter 3

Beginning Your Research
With the Indian Records

For many blacks with Indian Ancestry there is sometimes a misconception that the first *Indian* ancestor that will be found will be the *"full blood"* Indian. It is important to note that race was a significant factor with the Indians of the Five Civilized Tribes, and if there was any association with black people, the bloodline was frequently discounted by the time of the official enrollment of the Dawes Commission. This enrollment covered the late 1890s up to the time of Oklahoma statehood in 1907. The rolls are stated to be those documents created between 1898 and 1914, however, it is important to note that there were many political issues taking place at that time.

Enrollment in one nation was sometimes more complex than enrollment in another nation with the same commissioners being a part of the process. In the Cherokee Nation, the enrollment was based upon having been previously enrolled, or having a close relative previously enrolled on the 1880 authenticated Cherokee Census Roll. In the Chickasaw Nation, there was a roll created for Freedmen, including the same detailed interview process, although at the same time, the Chickasaw Nation did not adopt their Freedmen, officially.

Despite possible mixed heritage, many of the black citizens in Indian Territory, and their families were more likely to have been listed among the Freedmen. This should be understood. Did the Black Indians have Indian blood? Many did. However, the politics of the Dawes enrollment process, segregated many persons unfairly on different rolls, thus initiating a number of challenges to the rolls themselves, many of which continue into the 21st century.[1]

The lives of the Freedmen were totally immersed into Indian Territory culture, lifestyle and language. The lived among the Indians "by blood" and in many households, the Freedmen themselves were also "by blood." At the same time, the many Freedmen, were indeed former slaves of the wealthy slave owners in the nations and the critical task for the researcher is the separate the political status of the Freedmen, and when pursing the family history, to keep that focus in sight. The value of the genealogical data on the Dawes Freedmen records, cannot be emphasized enough, and will be demonstrated in following chapters.

When the Tribes submitted their final rolls those who were classified in their specific tribe had the "Freedmen" distinction. In other words, there were the Cherokee Freedmen, Choctaw Freedmen, Creek Freedmen, etc. The Seminole process was a seamless one that did not initially make a distinction between Freedmen and Seminoles "by blood". However, again politics later put the two Freedmen

---

[1] The Nero case in the 1980s challenged the practices in the Cherokee Nation. Bernice Riggs an African-Cherokee woman, born and raised in Tahlequah Oklahoma also unsuccessfully challenged the status of freedmen in Cherokee Court in the 1990s. Lucy Allen challenged the law again and won in 2006. In the Seminole Nation Sylvia Davis helped to regain status when the two Freedmen bands were voted back into the tribe after Federal funds were pulled in 2000.

The Cherokee Nation and Creek Nation have also had legal cases, with the case of Vann vs. Klempthorne and the Graham Johnson case in the Creek Nation. The case of Marilyn Vann et. al is a Freedman case, and the Graham Johnson case is one of blacks with ancestors on the blood roll challenging a tribe that removed black citizens from the nation by changing the constitution. Choctaw and Chickasaw Freedmen are now beginning to challenge their status as well.

bands that had always been full status citizens in the nation, on a Freedmen Roll, although they had always been simply two bands, equal to all other Seminole Bands.

Note that the lawsuits are not a recent development of the latter 20th century. Early on in the process, many "freedmen" designees challenged their placement on the roll, because they were a part of the Indian community into which they had been born, and raised. The cases of Choctaw children, Joe and Dillard Perry, and the Chickasaw case of Bettie Ligon each evolved into lengthy proceedings that covered many years.[2]

The Freedmen researcher should indeed research the records of the Indians "by blood", particularly because they will often find other members of the family who are on those rolls. However, since there are more than 20,000 Freedmen on the Dawes rolls, for a beginning of the process, these records are strongly recommended as a beginning.

It should be noted that there is a classification of Indians "by Marriage". They were often whites designated as *Intermarried Whites* who were also made citizens in the nation. There were in several cases, "state Negroes" meaning blacks who migrated into Indian Territory from the Deep South, who intermarried with Freedmen. The politics of the Dawes Commission stayed true to the many discriminatory practices of the neighboring United States. Thus the privilege

---

[2] Bettie Ligon was the primary plaintiff in what is now known *as Equity Case 7071*. She was the daughter of a Chickasaw leader, and was recognized by her father as his child, but still was placed on the Freedman rolls. Children of white mothers did not have this practice applied in their case. By the time the case ended there were several hundred persons who had joined the Ligon case. The story of Joe and Dillard Perry from the Choctaw Nation was equally involved and resulted in their getting on the blood roll, then taken off and then later put back.

of marrying into a nation was not extended to Freedmen spouses. A black person from Tennessee, who may have married someone from the Choctaw Nation, was not given citizenship, although a white person from Tennessee who married a citizen of the Choctaw Nation was given this privilege.

The Dawes Commission Process

Like all of the citizens of Indian Territory, the Freedmen went through essentially the same application process. This involved making the initial application, and going through a sometimes lengthy interview process in front of a panel of investigators known as the Dawes Commission. The purpose was to prepare the tribal rolls for each tribe. In order for all applicants, both citizens designated *"by blood"* and *"Freedmen"* to receive any kind of allotment of tribal lands, they had to go in fact through a lengthy process of interviews that in many cases took several years. In fact, it took on the average three to five years for a successful applicant to be enrolled by the Commission.

The records were divided into a variety of classifications, not just "By Blood" and "Freedmen." Note the following classifications:

♦**Cherokee Nation**
Cherokee by Blood
Cherokee Minors By Blood
Cherokee Minors
Delaware Indians (adopted by Cherokee Nation)
Cherokee by Marriage
Cherokee Freedmen
Cherokee Freedmen Minors

♦ **Choctaw Nation**
Choctaw by Blood
Choctaw New Born by Blood
Choctaw Minor By Blood
Choctaw Freedmen
Choctaw Minor Freedmen
Mississippi Choctaw by Blood
Mississippi Choctaw Minor by Blood

♦ **Chickasaw Nation**
Chickasaw by Blood
Chickasaw New Born by Blood
Chickasaw Minor by Blood
Chickasaw Freedmen
Chickasaw Freedmen Minor
Chickasaw Cancelled

♦ **Creek Nation**
Creek by Blood
Creek New Born by Blood
Creek Minor by Blood
Creek Freedmen
Creek Freedmen New Born, by Blood
Creek Freedmen Minor by Blood

♦ **Seminole Nation**
Seminole By Blood
Seminole New Born by Blood
Seminole Freedmen
Seminole Freedmen New Born by Blood

Within all of these classifications, the genealogist will find the three kinds of files that will be essential to their research. Each classification mentioned above has these file types that pertain them.

♦ **Enrollment Cards**
♦ **Application Jackets**
♦ **Final Rolls**

The ***Enrollment Cards*** consist of data pertaining to the applicants. The ***Application Jackets*** consist of interviews that were recorded during the process and the purpose of the entire series of interviews was to create, the ***Final Rolls.***

The Enrollment Cards

These cards are sometimes called "Census Cards." They actually contain information that is immediately of value to the genealogist. There is a distinction between the enrollment cards of the Indians "by blood" and those designated as "Freedmen". On the enrollment cards, there is the designation of "Blood Quantum". *(There are examples of these cards in the back of this book)* This supposedly represents a "degree of Indian blood", however this was made by conjecture, and in many cases by guessing. The Freedmen cards do not have this designation. The most unique feature of the Freedmen Enrollment cards is that of the identification of the Indian slave owner. This information is valuable to the genealogist. Note that to qualify for enrollment, the Freedmen had to have been a slave of a recognized Indian in the tribe, or the descendant of a slave of an Indian in the tribe. Some of these same Freedmen also had Indian blood. This is no surprise, since there were many former slaves in the Deep South who had the white blood of their white enslavers as well. When the Freedman had an Indian ancestor it was often noted on the cards as well.

On both types of cards, By Blood or Freedmen, the parentage is recorded. All applicants for enrollment, including the heads of household and their children had their own parents indicated. In the cases where there had been previous marriages, this data is extremely valuable, because the parents would not have been identified on any other kind of document.

Although Freedmen status did result in land allotment, it was significantly lower especially in the Choctaw and Chickasaw nations, than the lands given to those designated by blood. However, this status as Freedmen was still important. These citizens had to establish themselves as citizens of the Territory, and they had to distinguish themselves from "state blacks". By doing so, they would have proven the right to live on Indian Land, and to share in annuity payments. Most frequently in the Choctaw Nations, for example, the Freedmen allotments consisted of 40 acres, although Freedmen in other nations did receive 60 acres. Those designated by blood however, typically received 200-300 acres of land.[3]

By studying these cards the genealogist will be pleased to find in so many cases four "new ancestors" because the parents of those enrollees were usually listed. Also any person who was a slave had the name of the enslaver designated on the card. For many African American researchers, the effort to identify a slave owner can sometimes halt the research process for years. Meanwhile, these Freedmen cards provide this valuable data. The illustrations in chapters 5-8 illustrate this clearly.

Special Feature of Freedmen Cards

One feature of *Freedmen* cards is that they are typically two sided cards. Most cards *By Blood* and *New Born Cards* are one-sided cards with all data on the front.

---

[3] It should be noted that all persons in the Creek Nation received the same amount of land.

For the Freedman researcher, in the case of the Walton family,[4] the researcher gets a genealogical "gift" in the sense that four ancestors previously unknown are mentioned on this card. The parents of both Sallie and of Samuel are mentioned, on the card. The father of Sallie is stated to be Eastman Williams. He was not a slave at all, particularly because there is another column that specifies the name of the slave owner of each parent. With Eastman Williams, the card clearly indicates that he was not a slave, but was, in fact a Choctaw Indian himself. Her mother was 'Manda Hunt, whom it has already been indicated from the front side of the card, was formerly a slave of Emeline Perry. Both parents of Samuel Walton are also indicated. Pat Drenard and Lydia Walters. It appears that Lydia had been a slave and was formerly the slave of a Mrs. Walters. Although his father's surname is stated as Drenard, it is quite possible that "Walters" may have been the origin of the Walton family name

The Dawes records can give the researcher some clue to the number of times that freedmen changed their surnames. It was not uncommon for the freedman to use the name of a previous slave owner, or a different name completely and several different surnames for one person can sometimes be seen in the testimonies. In some families it was not until the early 20th century that the family surnames tended to remain unchanged.

These documents also emphasize the need to familiarize oneself with the geography of the Indian Territory. The counties and towns of contemporary Oklahoma did not exist in the Indian nations. For example in the Choctaw Nation, it was divided into three districts:

---

[4] See the Walton family documents and read the family interview in Chapter 6.

Moshulatubbee, Pushmataha, and *Apukshunubbee* Districts, which now no longer exist. They were subdivided into smaller counties such as *Sugar Loaf, Skullyville, Kiamitia* and *Atoka.* The area in which Samuel and Sallie Walton lived in is currently known as LeFlore County, yet when the family applied for enrollment, they resided in Skullyville County, near Oak Lodge, I.T. (Indian Territory). Today, Skullyville exists only as a Choctaw Indian cemetery outside the town of Spiro, in LeFlore County, Oklahoma.

Most of the enrollment cards are similar in each nation. In many cases if a spouse of child was not included on the card, a hand-written note reveals additional information for the family researcher. For example, on the card for Samuel Walton, his stepdaughter Louisa was 18 at the time of the application. However by the time the family was enrolled, she had married and had already had her first child. A hand-written reference to the enrollment of the child appears on the front side of the card. The reference directs the reader to "NB# 230" directing one to the New Born card # 230. This refers to the roll for minor children born to anyone on the primary file. Louisa's other children born after that time were subsequently added to the roll for New Born Choctaw Freedmen.

Location of the Freedmen Census Records

The original records pertaining to the Five Civilized Tribes are all kept in Ft. Worth, Texas at the Federal Records Center. However, they are also on microfilm at the National Archives in Washington D.C. and are accessible at most of the branches of the National Archives throughout the country. There are a large number of genealogical libraries throughout the country that also contain these records, and it is wise to check with the large research facilities throughout the country to see if microfilm copies are available.

Fortunately the microfilmed records can always be ordered directly from the National Archives as well.

The National Archives in Washington, D.C., has a locator directory, which assists the researchers in locating specific records. By referring to that directory, one will be directed to the appropriate cabinet containing the desired reel of microfilm. There are literally hundreds of rolls for each nation. Fortunately the reels are categorized by nation.

Microfilm Rolls Pertaining to Freedmen
M1186- The Enrollment Cards

Nation	Reel Number
Cherokee Freedmen	Reels 23-27 & 33-38
Choctaw Freedmen	Reels 50-53 & 55-56
Chickasaw Freedmen	Reels 70-75
Creek Freedmen	Reels 85-91
Seminole Freedmen	Reels 92-93

M1301 The Applications for Enrollment

The next five chapters will illustrate the structure and contents of the Application Jackets. These are the files that really contain the data pertinent to researchers. They tell much of the family history, though not all. The political nature of the Dawes Commission admitted some, denied others, and excluded many based on principles that are analyzed and discussed even to this day. However, the records are there to be utilized and are helpful in unraveling the family story.

Some of the files contain brief interviews that are simply one-sided statements. However, they still are useful for the data they provide. Others are lengthy exchanges between the enrollees and the Dawes Commissioners that provide some glimpses into the lives of the Freedmen. Some files also contain other kinds of data, including birth affidavits, death notices and occasionally marriage records. Therefore when working with Dawes files, M1301 is critical in one's work.

A word should be included here about a similar kind of record, which is also microfilmed at the National Archives Those are the records from publication **M1650.** The records are arranged by tribe and then application number. These records contain not only court proceedings but also useful information in affidavits, depositions, and family records.

Additional Freedman Records

In addition to the records mentioned about one will find earlier census records that were produced from 1867 to 1895 before the Dawes hearings actually began. There are records pertaining to the "colored" citizens of the various tribes, and are also useful in looking at in the family search. They are listed as follows:

Cherokee Nation
1867 Tompkins Roll
1880 Wallace Roll
1880 Cherokee Colored Persons Rolls
189-93 Wallace Roll of Cherokee Freedmen
1896 Cherokee Freedmen Census

Choctaw Nation
1885 Choctaw -Chickasaw Freedmen Rolls
1896 Choctaw- Chickasaw Census

Creek Nation
1867 Dunn Roll
1867 Creek Freedman Roll

1869 Pay roll of Creek Freedmen

Seminole Nation
Allotment Schedule for Seminoles

The Importance of Searching All Categories

As mentioned earlier, the genealogists would direct
his or her attention to all of the categories when looking for
ancestors because the same kind of information was
collected for each family, whether or not the application was
approved or denied. Some individuals may find their
ancestors on the Enrollment records, pertaining to the
citizens by blood. The primary difference between these
records and the freedmen enrollment cards is that there is no
blood quantum listed on the Freedmen cards. Later, on the
Final Tribal rolls, one will also note that the degree of Indian
blood is omitted there also.

The Omission of Indian Blood

The omission of Indian blood on the Freedmen
records has been discussed a great deal since the rolls were
created. The political structure of the Dawes Commission,
the population within the various tribes, and the monies
allotted to the various tribes are among the issues that were
at hand.[5] There was a good portion of the Freedmen
population that did have Indian blood, and their descendants

---

[5] The issue of Indian blood continues to this day with the various efforts
taking place by Freedmen descendants who make an effort to enroll in
the Cherokee Nation. In 2003 a lawsuit was filed against the BIA and its
policies of support of the Five Civilized Tribes to keep Freedmen from
enrolling the nations today. Freedmen groups have organized to
challenge these policies and are addressing the continuing biases against
enrolling its citizens of African ancestry.

often have more "Indian" blood than those who are enrolled today in the tribes. So this cannot be disputed that many freedmen were and are related to members of the tribes today.

However, the researcher should also remember that the original Freedmen are the former slaves of the Indians, and any recognition of blood ties to the Indians would be an admission of sexual contact that had been banned before and after Emancipation. These bans were later written into the constitution of the Nations. There was a also a difference in the resulting land allotments for those Indians who were enrolled as Indians by blood and those enrolled as Freedmen, so again, money, land and benefits came into the process. This distinction was indeed unfair and is the root cause of the political problems today with these five tribes.

The historical unfairness of the allotment process must be understood, while studying these records. Many will make the mistake of trying to prove and ancestor's "Indian blood" while ignoring the fact that their ancestors also had African blood, and this was what placed them politically in the Freedmen records. One must separate the unfairness of the process with the truth reflected regarding the parentage of the Freedmen. The genealogical process is a research based methodical process that should have objectivity as a basic element, and it is critical that the researcher maintain objectivity when researching these records.

There are a variety of records that should be utilized when exploring Indian Territory history and the African Americans within the Five Civilized Tribes. One must understand one fact----most blacks with ancestry in these nations will be found on the Freedmen records, and they are emphasized as a logical place to begin the research.

It is not uncommon for many beginning researchers to *insist* upon the full blood Indian status of their ancestors, which may indeed be the case. But the purpose for using the Freedmen records is the search for genealogical data on the family. The primary source of contact in Indian Territory between blacks and Indians was the institution of slavery.

This is not the case in states like Virginia, North and South Carolina, Georgia and Florida, but within the Territory that later became Oklahoma, it was slavery.[6] There were some cases where genuine friendships, courtships and marriages occurred, but until the end of the Civil War, the primary source of contact came through the enslavement of Africans by the Indians of the Five Civilized Tribes.

This point is emphasized because the opportunity to explore such documents is one of the few opportunities for African Americans to document a factual historic connection to any tribe of North American Indians. It is hoped that the researcher will not get lost in the quest for Indian blood, and lose sight of the genealogical value of the Freedmen records.

---

[6] There are still issues that prevail also in these same states with persons of African and Native American ancestry. The quest has been hampered for example in Virginia, by state registrar Walter Plecker who for decades personally took it upon himself to alter records of persons who had been listed originally in the records as Indians to have them re-classified as black.

Chapter 4

A Cherokee Case Study

The Pettit Family - Cherokee Freedmen

Chapter 4

A Cherokee Case Study
The Pettit Family - Cherokee Freedmen

The Black Indian researcher must utilize the Indian records, but also supplement this information with data taken from the Federal Census and if possible the Slave Narratives. The WPA slave narratives are the result of the 1930s Federal Writers project where former slaves shared their memories of their lives as slaves. The following case from the Cherokee Nation in Indian Territory, and it reveals an interesting balance for the researcher. The family documents are from the family of George Pettit who lived at the turn of the century Fort Gibson, Indian Territory. Almost three decades later, his wife Phillis was interviewed by the Federal Writers Project, and excepts from her interview are also included here. Note that in some cases there are differences in the spelling of the last name, therefore both Pettit and Petit are transcribed as they appear.

From M1301 Applications for Enrollment

Department of the Interior
Commission to the Five Civilized Tribes
Fort Gibson, I.T. April 4th 1901

In the matter of the application of George Pettit for the enrollment of himself, wife and three children as Cherokee Freedmen; said Pettit being sworn and examined by Commissioner T.B. Needles testified as follows:

Q. What is your name? A. George Pettit

Q. How old are you Mr. Pettit? A. About 54 years old.
Q. What is your post office? A. Fort Gibson.
Q. What district do you live in? A. Tahlequah.
Q. Do you apply to be enrolled as a Cherokee Freedman? A. Yes sir.
Q. Did you ever apply to be enrolled as a Freedman of any other Nation or tribe? A. No sir.
Q. Have you always been recognized as a Cherokee freedman by the authorities of the Cherokee Nation? A. Yes sir.
Q. Does your name appear upon the rolls of the Cherokee Nation? A. Yes sir.
Q. Who do you want to enroll besides yourself? A. My wife.
Q. Wife? A. Yes sir.
Q. How many children? A. Five.
Q. What is the name of your wife? A. Phillis
Q. Well about how old? A. I suppose about 49.
Q. What was her name when you married her? A. She was a Harnage.
Q. Was she a Cherokee Freedman? A. Yes sir.
Q. Please give me the names of your children, commencing with the oldest. A. Samuel Pettit, he is 25 years old.
Q. He will have to apply for himself. A. Sophie Pettit, she is 16.
Q. What is the name of the next one? A. Annie Pettit, she is about 11. Henry Pettit, he is not quite five, he is near five than he is four.
Q. Were you a slave during the war? A. Yes sir.
Q. What was your father's name? A. Tom Pettit
Q. Was he a Cherokee? A. Yes sir.
Q. Where were you at the beginning of the war between the United States and the Confederacy? A. Out here in Flint.[1]
Q. Did you go out? A. Yes sir.

---

[1] *Flint refers to the Flint District of the Cherokee Nation*

Q. When did you return? A. I returned August '66 about the first

Q. Have you been here ever since? A. Ever since. I ain't been out of the Nation.

Q. What was your wife's father's name? A. He was a Harnage, but his name is Thompson.

Q. What was her mother's name? A. Her mother's name was Tissie.

Q. Your wife was born after the war, I suppose? A. No sir, I suppose not.

Q. Is she your first wife? A. No sir, second.

Q. Is she the mother of your children? A. She is the mother of four of them.

Q. Is she the mother of Sophia, Annie and Henry? A. Yes sir.

Q. Has she always lived in the Cherokee Nation? A. Yes sir, raised here.

The 1880 Authenticated Roll of citizens of the Cherokee Nation[2] examined and the names of applicants found theron as follows:

| Page 792 | #1669 George Pettit, Tahlequah Dist. |
| Page 792 | #1670 Phillis Pettit, Tahlequah Dist. |

The 1896 Census roll of citizens of the Cherokee Nation examined and applicants names found thereon as follows:

Page 1318	#356	Phyllis Pettit, Tahlequah Dist.
Page 1318	#355	George Pettit, Tahlequah Dist.
Page 1318	#359	Sophie Pettit, Tahlequah Dist
Page 1318	#360	Annie Pettit, Tahlequah Dist
Page 1318	#362	Henry Pettit, Tahlequah Dist.

Q. Are these children alive? A. Yes sir.

Q. Living with you at this time? A. Yes sir.

---

[2] It should be noted that an extensive census was taken in the Cherokee Nation in 1880. Quite often one will find references to the 1880 list of "Authenticated" citizens.

COM'R NEEDLES–The names of George Pettit and his wife Phillis are found upon the authenticated roll of 1880 as well as the census roll of 1896. The names of his children, Sophia, Annie and Henry are found upon the census Roll of 1896. They are duly identified and make satisfactory proof as to residence, consequently George Pettit, and his wife Phillis and his children as named herein will be listed for enrollment as Cherokee Freedmen.

oooOOOooo

J. O. Rosson, being first duly sworn, states that as stenographer to the Commission to the Five Civilized tribes, he correctly recorded the testimony and proceedings in this case and that the foregoing is a true and complete transcript of his stenographic notes thereof.

Subscribed and sworn to before me this 4th day of April 1901.

T. B. Needles
Commissioner

- - - - - - - - - -

The previous interview is a good example of the kinds of questions that were asked by the Dawes Commission of Freedmen. There was an expectation that anyone who had left the nation during the Civil War that they return to their homes within six months time. That is why George Pettit's response about when he returned is significant. In addition, the significance of the wife's status as a member of the nation is also critical, as it was common practice to give any enrollment status to the children that mirrored the mother. It was clarified that Phillis Pettit was the mother of the children, and that just like their father, their mother was also a citizen on the tribe.

Note also that it is sometimes explained that the status of the mother having been a slave is justification for the children to have been enrolled as Freedmen, even when the father may have been of Native ancestry. There are many cases in the territory where persons obtained Native blood through their father's line and they were given status on the rolls "by blood". If one has African and Indian ancestry, this was most often not applied. This double standard is among the issues currently being challenged today in the Cherokee, Creek and Seminole nations. The Choctaw and Chickasaw nations do not have current lawsuits confronting them, although many within the nations are aware and are watching the developments in Oklahoma in the other tribes.

The George Pettit case is also significant, because they were slaves of prominent Cherokees. Typically, those enslaved by Cherokees of status, seldom had major challenges towards their enrollment as Freedmen, by the Commission.

The Phillis Pettit Interview in the WPA Slave Narratives

The value of the slave narratives is well known to African ancestored genealogists. These interviews were conducted in the late 1930s as part of the Federal Writer's Project of the Works Projects Administration. What is not widely known, is that there were a series of interviews conducted in the state of Oklahoma of persons who had been slaves of the Indians of the Five Civilized Tribes. Phillis Pettit was among the persons interviewed. The story of her life as a slave is a valuable tool for the family historian, and for anyone studying Indian Territory history. To enhance the data on the Pettit family, this is a wonderful resource to include, that puts more flavor and substance to the family history. The interview of Phillis Pettit appears below.

I was born in Rusk County Texas, on a plantation about eight miles east of Belleview. There wasn't no town where I was born, but they had a church.

My mammy and pappy belonged to a part Cherokee named W. P. Thompson where I was born. He had kinfolks in the Cherokee Nation, and we all moved up here to a place of Fourteen Mile Creek close to where Hulbert now is, way before I was big enough to remember anything. Then, so I been told, old master Thompson sell my pappy and mammy and one of my baby brothers and me back to one of this neighbors in Texas name of John Harnage.

Mammy's name was Letitia Thompson and Pappy's was Riley Thompson. My little brother was named Johnson Thompson, but I had another brother sold to Vann and he always call hisself (sic)Harry Vann. His Cherokee master lived on the Arkansas river close to Webber's Falls and I never did know him until we was both grown. My only sister was Patsy and she was borned (sic) after slavery and died at Wagoner, Oklahoma.

I can just remember when master John Harnage took us to Texas. We went in a covered wagon with oxen and camped out all along the way. Mammy done the cooking in big wash kettles and pappy done the driving of the oxen. I would set in a wagon and listen to him pop his whip and holler.

Master John took us to his plantation and it was big one, too. You could look from the field up to the Big House and any grown body in the yard look like a little body, it was so far away.

We Negroes lived in quarters not far from the Big House and ours was a single log house with a stick and dirt chimney. We cooked over the hot coals in the fireplace.

I just played around until I was about six years old I reckon, and then they put me up at the Big House with my mammy to work. She done all the cording and spinning and weaving, and I done a whole lot of sweeping and minding the baby. The baby was only about six months old, I reckon. I used to stand by the cradle and rock it all day, and when I quit I would go to sleep right by the cradle sometimes before mammy would come and get me.

The Big House had great big rooms in front, and they was fixed up nice too. I remember when old Mrs. Harnage tired me out sweeping up the front rooms. They had two or three great big pictures of some old people hanging on the wall. They was full blood Indians it look like, and I was sure scared of them pictures! I would go here and there and every which-a-way, and anywheres I go them big pictures always looking straight at me and watching me sweep! I kept my eyes right on them so I could run if they moved, and old Mistress take me back to the kitchen and say I can't sweep because I miss all the dirt.

We always have good eating, like turnip greens cooked in a kettle with hog skins and crackling grease, and skinned corn, and rabbit or possum stew. I like big fish tolerable well too, but I was afraid of the bones in the little ones.

That skinned corn ain't like the boiled hominy we have today. To make it you boil some wood ashes, or have some drip lye from the hopper to put in the hot water. Let the corn boil in the lye water until the skin drops off and the eyes drop out and then wash that corn in fresh water about a dozen times or just keep carrying water from the spring until you are wore out, like I did. Then you put the corn in a crock and set it in the spring, and you got good skinned corn as long as it last, all ready to warm up a little batch at time.

Master had a big, long log kitchen setting away from the house, and we set a big table for the family first, and when they was gone we negroes at the house eat at that table too, but we don't use the china dishes

The Negro cook was Tilda Chisholm. She and my mammy didn't do no outwork. Aunt Tilda sure could make them corn-dodgers. Us children would catch her eating her dinner first out of the kettles and when we say something she say" "Go on child, I jest tasting that dinner." In the summer we had cotton homespun clothes, and in winter it had wool mixed in. They was dyed with copperas and wild indigo.

My brother, Johnson Thompson, would get up behind old Master Harnage on his horse and go with him to hunt squirrels. Johnson would go 'round on the other side of the tree, and rock the squirrels so they would go 'round on Master's side so's he could shoot them. Master's old mare was named, "Old Willow" and she knowed how to stop and stand real still so he could shoot.

His children was just all over the place! He had two houses full of them! I only remember Bell, Ida, Maley, Mary and Will, but they was plenty more I don't remember.

That old horn blowed 'way before daylight, and all the field Negroes had to be out in the row by the time of sun up. House Negroes got up too, because old Master always up to see everybody get out to work.

Old Master Harnage bought and old slaves most all the time, and some of the new Negroes always acted up and needed a licking. The worst ones got beat up good, too! They didn't have no jail to put slaves in because when the Masters got done licking them they didn't need no jail.

My husband was George Petit. He tell me his mammy was sold away from him when he was a little boy. He looked down a long lane after her just as long as he could see her, and cried after her. He went down to the big road and set down by his mammy's barefooted tracks in the sand, and set there until it got dark, and then he come on back to the quarters.

I just saw one slave try to get away right in hand. They caught him with bloodhounds and brung him back in. The hounds had nearly tore him up, and he was sick a long time. I don't remember his name, but he wasn't one of the old regular Negroes.

In Texas we had a church where we could go. I

think it was a white church and they just let the Negroes have it when they got a preacher sometimes. My mammy took me sometimes, and she loved to sing them salvation songs.

We used to carry news from one plantation to the other I reckon, 'cause momma would tell about things going on some other plantation and I know she never been there.

Christmas morning we always got some brown sugar candy or some molasses to pull, and we children was up bright and early to get that 'lasses pull, I tell you! And in the winter we played skeeting on the ice when the water froze over. No, I don't mean skating. That's when you got iron skates, and we didn't have them things. We just get a running start and jump on the ice and skeet as far as we could go, and then you run some more.

I nearly busted my head open, and brother Johnson said: "Try it again, " but after that I was scared to skeet any more.

Mammy say we was down in Texas to get away from the War, but I didn't see any war and any soldiers. But one day old Master stay after he eat breakfast and when us Negroes come in to eat he say" After today I ain't your master any more. You all as free as I am." We just stand and look and don't know what to say about it.

After a while Pappy got a wagon and some oxen to drive for a white man who was coming to the Cherokee Nation because he had folks here. His name was Dave Mounts and he had a boy named

John.

We come with them and stopped at Fort Gibson where my own grandmammy was cooking for the soldiers at the garrison. Her name was Phyllis Brewer and I was named after her. She had a good Cherokee master. My mammy was born on his place.

We stayed with her about a week and then we moved out on Four Mile Creek to live. She died on Fourteen-Mile Creek about a year later

When we first went to Four Mile Creek, I seen Negro women chopping wood and asked them who they work for and I found out they didn't know they was free yet.

After a while my pappy and mammy both died, and I was took care of by my aunt Elsie Vann. she took my brother Johnson, too, but I don't know who took Harry Vann.

I was married to George Petite, and I had on a white underdress and black high top shoes, and a large cream colored hat, and on top of all I had a blue wool dress with tassles all around the bottom of it. That dress was for me to eat the terrible supper in. That what we called the wedding supper because we eat too much of it. Just danced all night too! I was at Mandy Foster's house in Fort Gibson and the preacher was Reverend Barrows. I had that dress a long time, but it's gone now. I still got the little sun bonnet I wore to church in Texas.

We had six children, but all are dead but George,

Tish and Annie now.

Yes, they tell me Abraham Lincoln set me free, and I love to look at his picture on the wall in the school house at Four Mile branch where they have church. My grand mammy kind of help start that church, and I think everybody ought to belong to some church.

I want to say again my Master Harnage was Indian, but he was a good man and mighty good to us slaves, and you can see I am more than six feet high and they way I weighs over a hundred and sixty, even if my hair is snow white.

This interview is very significant for many reasons. The life of both Phyllis and her husband as slaves is reflected in her narrative. She reveals that the Cherokee slaves, like slaves in the Deep South, lived in fear of being sold away from parents, and loved ones as she recounted the story of her husband, watching his mother being sold. Phillis Pettit described a well developed southern slave culture that she lived in. A "big house" was there with slave quarters, with both house and field slaves. Some slaves were beaten, and as she described their lives, *"They didn't have no jail to put slaves in because when the masters got done licking them they didn't need no jail."*

The Cherokee nation was the largest, tribe in the Territory, and the largest number of Freedmen records are found from that nation. The combination of records from the Dawes Commission, Census records as well as the Slave Narratives should all be used when documenting this unique history.

70

Chapter 5
Creek Case Studies

Intertwined Families-By Blood
And Freedmen Together

Chapter 5

Intertwined Creek Families---
By Blood and Freedmen together.

The Muskogee Creek Nation offers an interesting foray into the complexity of families during 19th and early 20th century history. The Dawes records from the Creek Nation might appear to be fragmented by the fact that a good portion of the records are missing, however, the complicated structure can still be analyzed by a close study of what does remain. [1]

There are two valuable sources of information about the Creek Nation. The Old Series cards, never microfilmed, but still available for research by the southwest branch of the National Archives. The other more available source of data comes from the Census Cards, found on National Archives publication M1186. The Freedmen cards contain some of the same data highlighted in the missing interviews, and it only takes the tenacious researcher to put together some of the data.

---

[1] The National Archives did not microfilm all of the Creek Nation interviews, for reasons never disclosed. There are many theories, all unproven as to what happened to the records. There are rumors of the destruction of the records by tribal officials, other rumors claim that the records were not destroyed, but merely hidden, by the same persons. The interviews themselves, which might highlight family relationships, are believed to have "escaped" the microfilming process because of the mixed blood nature of a large portion of the nation. The "admixture" of concern is said, to be the African-Creek mixture, which created alarm that too much presence of black blood might turn the BIA against the tribe. This aversion to the presence of black blood has continued into the 21st century, although a sizeable portion of the enrolled nation is already mixed African and Creek.

Researcher and genealogist Tonia Holleman, of Van Buren Arkansas, has studied some of the relationships between families that can be gleaned from the Dawes Enrollment cards. Her findings are highlighted in the following section. The significance of the information is that there is a clear blood tie between Creeks by Blood and Creek Freedmen, where in many cases, there was simply instruction by Dawes Commissioners to put a person, who was the child of a Creek by blood, on the Freedman roll. This status on the Freedman roll had few implications at the time for Creeks, since all Creeks got land and per capita payments.

However, 100 years after the rolls have closed, history and politics have now crossed, with the disenfranchisement of thousands of persons on the Freedmen rolls. This alienation occurred in the other tribes as well, however, the Creek Nation's expelling of the Freedmen was in direct contrast to the plethora of families that were mixed, and a part of the leadership of the tribe---perhaps more than all of the other tribes. Closeness that once was, has now evolved into a fear of any admission of having black relatives, ancestors, and in some cases, friends.

This oddity of blatant aversion to blacks, in spite of a history to the contrary, is worth examining. The treatment of blacks differently by the Creeks was encouraged, condoned and even urged, by the commissioners on the Dawes commission. Blood quantum whether present or not, was simply not recorded on census cards for freedmen. This was the case in all of the five nations. Blood quantum did not have to be recorded with Intermarried Whites, since there was no Indian blood to record. However, since there is no aversion to children who descend from Intermarried whites, the lack of Indian blood in these cases is overlooked. With all of the tribes, including the Creeks, the US government agency, the BIA is now the government body that issues the key to enrollment for many whose ancestors are on the Dawes Rolls----a CDIB card. The CDIB, which stands for Certificate of Degree of Indian Blood, relies on how one's blood was recorded on a list---the Dawes lists.

Although one does not and cannot "measure" blood, this politically motivated list, and one's ancestor's placement on that list, is now structured to police out any undesirables who were on a portion of that same list. The tribes now use this list with racial distinction, to determine who is eligible for tribal membership today. The BIA which bases the issuance of CDIB cards, on this illegally structured list, reinforces the disenfranchisement of persons on the Freedmen rolls, although ironically, by relying on the CDIB cards, the BIA also places the same nations in jeopardy of "measuring" themselves out of existence.

In the Creek Nation, what took place were dozens of families being divided by complexion in many cases. A few such cases are outlined here. This section is followed by a case study of the Sullivan family found on the few remaining Creek interviews.

Creek Parents, Freedmen Children—All One Family[2]

<u>SUNNY GRAYSON</u>—**Creek by Blood Census Card-607**, Sunny Grayson's daughter (Vicy Dansby) is listed as ¼ Blood and on Creek by Blood Census Card-823, another daughter (Lou Johnson) is listed as ¼ Blood. Sunny Grayson is on the Freedman Roll-Census Card 400-Roll number #1586 with his Freedman family and wife. The half

---

[2] This information was researched by Tonia Holleman of Van Buren Arkansas, December 2005.

sisters of Vicy and Lou are not on the roll because of a different mother. This shows a child or children of a Black father can be on Creek by Blood but does not show how much Black quantum.

ROBERT BRUNER-Census Card-#2383-Creek by Blood Roll Number-7132—list Robert Bruner as Full Blood. **Robert Bruner- Census Card 1994-Creek by Blood-list a Robert Bruner as father of Judy Bruner, daughter of Lizzie Harjo.** Judy is listed as Full Blood. Note-----There are _two_ Robert Bruner's on the Creek by Blood. Each one is listed as Full Blood. So therefore, the Robert Bruner listed as father on the Freedman Roll is Full Blood Creek.

GEORGE LEWIS – Freedman Census Card 405, Roll number on Freedman Roll-1602 and a daughter, Sarah Ann Lewis #1603, should be given ½ Creek Blood for George Lewis, who's alias is George Bruner: Sarah Ann Lewis should be given ¼ Creek Blood due to her Grandfather Robert Bruner being Full Blood.

JESSE BRUNER – Creek by Blood Census Card-1426- Roll number-#4544 – married Creacy Island, a freedwoman. Jesse Bruner is listed as ½ Creek by Blood. Therefore his children listed on the Freedman Roll should be given ¼ Creek by Blood and placed on the Creek by Blood Roll. [Further research may show Creacy Island will have some degree of Creek Blood.]

LUCY BRUNER–Freedman Roll-Census Card 418-Roll number #1651, married a Mose Grayson. Lucy should be listed as ¼ Creek by Blood and placed on the Creek by Blood Roll. (Lucy is the daughter of Jesse Bruner and Creacy Island, listed above.)

JAMES HAYNES-Creek by Blood Census Card-#1871-Roll Number-#5925-is listed as Full Blood. He married Louisa Grayson, a Freedman. Therefore their children are all listed on the Freedman Roll but <u>are ½ Creek by Blood and not on the Creek by Blood Roll</u>. They were penalized and placed on Freedman rolls due to their mother being a Black Indian.

RENTY or RENTIE- Census Card #1565 list Renty as Full Blood. Viewing Freedmen Roll of Creek Nation – Solomon Rentie is the son of Renty Full Blood. Renty #1565 married Phyllis Yargee the Slave of Cat Yargee. Solomon was not recorded on Creek by Blood <u>as being ½ or his children who are ¼ Creek by Blood.</u>

SALLY HUDSON- This one card is very interesting. On Sally's Census Card 433-Freedman Roll Number -#1719. There are comments on the card about her father. It states **Jim Yargee**, **Creek by Blood** but Sally Yargee Hudson is not on the CREEK BY BLOOD as ½. Why? Jim Yargee married Bettie Rentie, a black Indian Freedman and Sally is ½ Black. Betty Rentie Yargee then married **SUGAR T. GEORGE**[3]

JULIA JEFFERSON MORRISON- Freedman Roll Census Card-#446-Roll Number 1751- Julia's father was Thomas Jefferson-Creek by Blood Census Card 217; list Thomas and his Creek Wife and Children all as Full Blood. Thomas Jefferson-CC #217 marries Phillis McGilbray, a Black Indian. Their daughter Julia Jefferson Morrison should be on Creek by Blood as ½ but was denied her heritage

---

[3] Sugar T. George is the same person who served in the House of Kings in the Creek Nation for many years in the 1870s 1880s and 1890s. He was a major presence in the Muskogee Creek Nation, but now unidentified and not honored by his nation today.

because of her Black Indian Mother and her half-brother and sisters enjoyed the full benefits of the Creek Nation.

LIZZIE TURNER- Freedman Roll Census Card-#1099-Roll Number-#4153- Lizzie's father was MOSE PERRYMAN, Full Blood Creek. Lizzie should be listed as ½ Creek, and her children, ¼, and her grandchildren 1/8 Creek. Her mother was a Black Indian, Tempsey Canard.

* * * * *

These ten small cases are mere examples of the complexity of the families within the Creek Nation. With the reliance on the government sanctioned BIA and the CDIB cards, the aversion to the African admixtures actually found in many Creek families, the nation and the community has resorted to hiding traces of black ancestry on many levels. Persons of influence within the tribe have for many years resorted to denying their own family legacy, for fear of discovery by officials who might have a different response to the nation. With now more than a generation having passed since the interviews were "lost" and never microfilmed, the subsequent generations are being taught that their ancestor's lives that were once intermingled between three races, never happened and that the contact with "others" in the family were primarily white.

Fortunately, for the family historian, the destruction was not complete, the census cards do remain and other family relations can be explored and analyzed in spite of tribal unavailability. In fact, the census cards are presented clearly in a matter of fact manner, without the emotional flavor found in interviews, and the objectivity of the presentation of data in the Creek Census Cards makes them even more valuable as a research tool.

A Creek Case Study

Andrew Sullivan, Creek Freedman

This case is interesting in that Andrew Sullivan, lived his entire life with Muskogee Creek people from the period before removal and remained in Indian Territory the remainder of his life. He applied for enrollment with the Dawes Commission in 1900, but details about his life in the Territory give reference to his having received payments over the years as a Creek citizen. The complexities of life in the Territory after the war, of moving back into the Territory, of the various payments made to citizens of the nation through the post civil war years, all are reflected in this interview. In addition the process was still one for those within the nation, of having to prove not only one's presence in the Nation, but also the requirement to verify the legitimacy of the family was often brought out during the Dawes Commission interviews.

* * * * * * * * * *

DEPARTMENT OF THE INTERIOR
COMMISSION TO THE FIVE CIVILIZED TRIBES
MUSKOGEE LAND OFFICE, April 18, 1900

In the Matter of the Application of
Andrew Sullivan and his daughter Sarah
for enrollment of the Creek Nation

———

BEFORE THE COMMISSION TO THE FIVE CIVILIZED
TRIBES

Andrew Sullivan, being first duly sworn testified as follows:
Q. What is your name. A. Andrew Sullivan
Q. How old are you? A. About eighty years – about 82.

79

Q. What town do you belong to? A. Belong to Arkansas.[4]
Q. What is your post office address? A. Muskogee
Q. Do you consider yourself a citizen of the Creek Nation?
A. If I ain't you won't find another one here.
Q. You do then? A. Yes sir.
Q. How long have you resided in the Creek Nation? A. I was born in the Creek Nation.
Q. Have you lived here all your life? A. Yes, backwards and forward, all my life.
Q. I ask how long have you lived in the Creek nation? A. That's what I am trying to tell you. I have been living here over forty years or more. Ever since I came to this country. I come here when I was twenty years old.
Q. Then you weren't born in the Creek Nation? A. Yes, in Alabama, in the Creek Nation with the Injuns; I come here with them.
Q. How long did you live in Alabama? A. About 20 years when I left Alabama and come here.
Q. When did you come to the Indian Territory? A. I can't tell you that. I can't read. I can tell you who carried me here. Captain Rummel, he brought me out with the Injuns.(sic)
Q. Did you come with a lot of Injuns and colored people? A. Yes sir.
Q. You don't know when that was? A. Yes sir.
Q. Was it long before the war? A. Yes way before the war. I left Alabama when I was about 20 years old to come out to the Indian Territory.
Q. You lived in the state of Alabama in the Creek Nation until you were about 20 years old and then came to the Indian Territory? A. Yes

---

[4] Arkansas, sometimes referred to ask Arkansas Colored Town, was one of several all black towns in Indian Territory. This was one of the 27 all black communities that would exist in Oklahoma prior to statehood. Eventually the town would disappear, after statehood.

Q. Have you resided in the Indian Territory ever since? A. Ever since, only for going out and coming.

Q. Where did you go when you first come to the Territory? A . Way up on the other side of Eufala about 15 miles on the Canadian.[5]

Q. Did you go out of the Indian Territory after you came here?

A. No, I stayed right around her and then got to freight backwards and forwards. I was a regular teamster before the war.

Q. You didn't go out of the Territory before the war? A. Go out and come I as tell you with a team.

Q. Where did you go to when you went out of the Territory? A. I went to Ft. Smith, and back here to Gibson.

Q. How long have you lived in Ft. Smith? A. I didn't live there at all. I stayed there until I got my pension working and then come back.

Q. Didn't' you go to Texas during the war? A.Yes, me and Paterson here, I freighted for him.

Q. How long did you remain n Texas? A. It took me about 10 days to go and pretty much the same to come. I hauled in Texas for Paterson.

Q. Did you ever live in Texas? A. No sir.

Q. You have simply been a transient man, moving back and forth? A. I was a regular teamster.

Q. You have always made your residence since you came here sixty years ago, in the Indian Territory? A. Yes sir.

Q. At what place? A. At Eufala way upon the Canadian, and from Eufala down here. I lived across the river here about four years, and made a crop for Mahardy.

Q. Have you ever been married? A. Yes sir.

---

[5] The Canadian refers to the Canadian River that runs through Oklahoma.

Q. More than once? A. About three times. My wife died, I first stayed with, she died south, then I come here and married again, and she's dead, and I married again, so that is three dead.

Q. Did you have any children from the third wife? A. No, just a child from the second.

Q. Which one did you have a child by? A. That one. Becky Smith is my daughter. She is married.

Q. She was a daughter by your second wife? A. Yes sir.

Q. Did you have any children from the third wife? No sir.

Q. What was the name of the third wife? Rene Sullivan.

Q. Did you have any children by that wife? A. No Sir.

Q. Have you a daughter by the name of Sarah Sullivan? A. Yes sir.

Q. Who was the mother of that child? A. Her mother was at Ft. Smith.

Q. What was her name? A. Mollie

Q. Was Mollie a citizen of the Creek Nation? A. No, we parted.

Q. Were you married to Mollie? A. Yes sir.

Q. How long did you live with her? A. About two years, and took care of her.

Q. Is Mollie now living? A. I don't know.

Q. You say Rene was your last wife did you? A. Yes sir.

Q. And that you have a daughter that is married by the name of Becky Smith, and Rene was your last wife? A. Yes sir.

Q. Then you come here with a child by the name of Sarah, and you say Mollie is her mother. How could you be married to her, and Rene at the same time? A. Her name was Mollie— this child's mother. Rene was my last wife. I had this child between Mollie and Rene before I had Rene.

Q. Were you married by a minister to the mother of Sarah. A. No, just the way they married then.

Q. You simply lived together as man and wife? A. Yes, sir.

Q. I want to understand you fully, what is the name of Sarah's mother? A. Mollie.

Q. What was her other name? A. I don't know. Never asked her that. I just knowed Mollie.

Q. Is she dead? A. I can't tell you; I don't know, it has been so long.

Q. Patsy was the mother of Betsy? A. Yes sir.

Q. How old is Betsy Smith? A. She is about 50 or 60.

Q. I don't understand how, if you had a child by the name of Betsy by your last wife who is now 60 yeas old, how you could have this child. A. That was way before the war. Mrs. Smith was married before the war; she has got grandchildren 20 years old.

Q. How long did you live with Mollie? A. Long time–about 20 some odd years.

Q. Since you lived with her? And she is the mother of Sarah? A. No, about 14 years; Sarah is going on 14 years.

Q. You will have to bring better proofs than you have here, to show that Sarah is a legitimate child, and it appears further that mother of Sarah was not a citizen of the Creek Nation, and it is our opinion that Sarah is not entitled to enrollment. Have you participate in the different payments in the Creek Nation?

A. Yes, I got every dollar that was ever paid.

Q. Did you draw the money on the Dunn roll payment?

A. I'll tell you who drawed it. I didn't get it, old man Durant, my chief go tit, and told me "I have got you money you must come up and see them." I was living at the point, and before I come and seen the old man, he was dead and buried, and I lost that;. That is all the money I lost.

Q. Did you draw what is called the bread moncy? A. Yes sir.

Q. How much did you get at that time? A. $8. $4 for me and $4 for my wife.

Q. Did you draw the $29 in '90? A. Yes sir.

Q. For how many? A. For the three of us.

Q. For yourself, wife and daughter? A. Yes sir.

Q. Did you draw the money in 1895–$14? Yes, I can prove that by Mr. Seevers.

Q. You drew that for yourself and Sarah? Q. Yes, and took it up to Mr. Seevers.

Q. Did you ever go any other name than Andrew Sullivan? A. No sir.

Dick Carr, begin first duly sworn testified as follows:

Q. What town do you belong to? A. Arkansas

Q. What is your post office? A. Checota.

Q. Are you a citizen of the Creek Nation? A. Yes sir.

Q. By blood or adoption? A. Adoption

Q. Is your name on the Dunn Roll? A. Yes sir.

Q. Do you know that Sarah is his daughter?

Q. Yes, that is what I can't say only what he said.

Q. How long have you known Sullivan? A. I have known him to my recollection about 17 years.

Q. Has he resided in the Creek Nation during all the time you have known him? A. In part; he was here back and forth as he says.

Q. Where did he reside during the other part? A. He would go from one place to another; to Ft. Smith and back here.

Q. He was sort of transient, moving back and forth? A. I suppose so.

Q. Do you know of your own knowledge whether or not he claimed his residence to be in Ft. Smith or Indian Territory? A. Indian Territory.

Q. Didn't he ever reside in Ft. smith? With his wife and family? A. Yes, sir

Q. Do you know how long he resided there with them? A. Not exactly. Near as I can remember, about a year; maybe a little longer, maybe not quiet as long.

Q. Do you know about when that was? A. It was about the time of this $29 payment.

Q. The $29 in 1890? A. Yes sir.

Q. How many of his family did you draw for? A. For himself and girl and wife.

Q. What was the name of his wife at that time? A. Rene Sullivan

Q. Did you draw the $29 for Andrew Sullivan, his wife, Rene and daughter Sarah Sullivan? A. Yes sir.

Q. Do you know anything about a wife of his named Mollie? Do you know whether or not Rene was the mother of this child, Sarah? A. No, she was not.

Q. You drew this money at the time you drew for your own family? A. Yes, sir.

Q. Did you include in your family list, these three names? A. I believe it was on the same page, If I am not mistaken.

Q. Did you ever draw any money for Benny Selinus? A. No sir.

Q. Was there any member of your family names, Selinus? A. I don't know any of them at tall of that name. It is a new thing on me.

Q. You drew money for Lewis Carr, David, C. Carr, Nannie Carr Tupper, Winnie Tupper and Melinda Barnet? A. Melinda Barnet drawed her own money.

Q. Did you draw for the others I mentioned? A. Yes, sir.

Q. And delivered the money to him? A. Yes, sir.

Department of the Interior
Commissioner to the Five Civilized Tribes

I certify that My official oath as a stenographer to above named Commission that this transcription is a free full and correct translation of my stenographic notes.

Francis R. Bronson
(his signature)

85

Chapter 6

A Choctaw Case Study
Samuel & Sallie Walton
Choctaw Freedmen

Chapter 6

A Choctaw Case Study

The Family of Samuel and Sallie Walton - Choctaw Freedmen

This case appears to be a simple one, where the family of Samuel Walton, was admitted to the Choctaw Nation. Samuel Walton had been a slave of Jim Davis who had married into the Nail Family. Sallie, his wife was born in the Choctaw Nation, and her mother Amanda ('Manda) had been a slave to Emeline Perry. Sallie's daughter from a previous marriage was living with Samuel and Sallie at the time, and like her parents, she was admitted without difficulty. The enrollment cards of both Sallie and Samuel reflect that from the time of the application in 1899, to official approval and enrollment in 1904, that Sallie's daughter had then married. Information on the grandchild was also available for further family research.

This case is significant, because it was the Walton family history that initiated this author's research into the Dawes records. Since Sallie's Walton's death did not occur until 1961, there are many in the family who have a strong memory of her to this day. This family file, is also significant, because 8 years after the first family file was located in the Dawes Records, in1991, a letter, long lost among family documents, surfaced. This letter was written to Sallie, in 1923, and the hand written letter revealed even more information about her family history. Sallie's mother is already identified on the enrollment card as 'Manda. The family Bible recorded her as Amanda. The interview identifies her mother as being Amanda Anoatubby, or

Anchatubby, depending on the interpretation of the handwriting. The old letter –transcribed and included in this text–confirms Amanda as her mother, and the letter also identifies Amanda's parents thus providing the names of Sallie's grandparents. Sallie's grandfather was James Crow, a Choctaw Indian himself and is revealed in the letter.

There are many lessons from this one file. It is essential that the researcher pay close attention to the notes on the bottom of the enrollment cards, which in this case led to the Sallie's daughter's file. Secondly, the family documents are always important. An old letter, which remained in the hands of Sallie's only living granddaughter, till 1999, provided what might have been long lost information. The names of Sallie's grandparents, are mentioned and there would have been no way, in existing, records, to have connected Sallie Walton, to her grandparents, James and Kitty Crow.

The enrollment interviews and the letter follow. The Walton family appears on Choctaw Freedman Card No. 777. The daughter Louisa married Rev. George Sanders, and the interview to admit the children appears on Choctaw Freedmen New Born No. 230.

* * * * *

In re the application of Sam Walton to the Commissioner to the Five Civilized Tribes at Spiro, I.T. June 12th 1899, for enrollment as a Choctaw Freedman, being duly sword and examined by Commissioner Needles, he testified as follows:

Q. What is your name? A. Sam Walton
Q. How old are you? A. About fifty-six
Q. Were you born a slave? A. Yes sir.

Q. Who was your master? A. Josiah Harrell
Q. Where were you born? A. In Arkansas.
Q. Where were you at the time of the surrender?[1] A. In the Choctaw Nation.
Q. Where have you lived since then? A. Right in the Nation. Ever since. I have been out of the Nation on business but my home has always been in the Territory.
Q. Did your master bring you from Arkansas over here? A. He sold me over here.
Q. Who to? A. Jim Davis
Q. What was Jim Davis? A. Choctaw.

W.A. Welch being duly sworn testified as follows:
Q. What is your name? A. W.A. Welch
Q. Do you know this man Sam Walton? A. Yes sir.
Q. Do you know whose slave he was before the surrender? A. I am not very definite about that, but my memory is that he belonged to Jim Davis.
Q. Do you know where he has lived since the surrender? A. No sir.

Sam Davis re-examined.[2]
Q. Are you married? A. Yes sir.
Q. What is your wife's name? A. Sallie Walton

Sallie Walton being duly sworn testified as follows:

Q. What is your name? A. Sallie Walton
Q. Who did your mother belong to? A. Gilbert Perry
Q. What was he a Choctaw or Chickasaw? A. Choctaw.
Q. What was your mother's name? A. Amanda Anchatubbee

---

[1] The "surrender" refers to the surrender of Gen. Lee, at Appomattox that ended the Civil War.

[2] The document refers to Samuel as Davis, though Samuel used the name of Walton in the interview and in his personal life.

(Requested to bring further proof before enrollment.)

Dept. of the Interior
Commission to the Five Civilized Tribes

In re the application for Sam Walton for enrollment Dick
Brashears being duly sworn testified as follows:

Q. What is your name? A. Dick Brashears
Q. How old are you? A. Going on 79.
Q. Just state what you know about Sam Walton and where he
has been. A. Every time I saw him, he was in the Choctaw
Nation. He belonged to a white man by the name of
JimDavis. He married into the Nail Family. Jonathan Nail's
sister.
Q. You are certain that he was owned by Jim Davis? A. He
was there, and called him Master Jim.
Q. What is his profession? A. He is a preacher.
Q. And goes here and there and preaches everywhere? A.
Yes sir.
Q. You don't know that he ever lived out of the nation? A.
No he never lived anywhere that I know of except in the
Choctaw and Chickasaw Nation.

*(Requested to get further proof as to his wife, and both be
enrolled together.)*

Dept. of the Interior
Commission to the Five Civilized Tribes

Red Oak, I.T. June 20th 1899

In re enrollment of Sallie Walton
Nail Perry being duly sworn testifies as follows:
Q. What is your name? A. Nail Perry

Q. How old are you? A. Sixty four.
Q. Do you know Sallie Walton? A. Yes sir. I know her.
Q. Do you know who she was freed under? A. The mother of Sallie Walton was freed under my sister, Emeline Perry.
Q. Was your sister a Choctaw? A. Yes sir.
Q. She was freed here in the Choctaw Nation was she? A. Yes, sir.
Q. Do you know whether she has any children or not? A. I don't know what children she has, but she had about three the last I knew anything of her.
Q. She was here in the Choctaw Nation at the time of Freedom was she? A. Yes sir, she was a very small child she was still a sucking child at that time.

Sam Walton re-examined:
Sam Walton: I have a step daughter my wife's daughter I want to enroll.
Q. What is her name? A. Louisa Ingram
Q. Has she any children? A. No sir.
Q. She is a daughter of your present wife, is she? A. Yes sir.

Enrolled Sam Walton, his wife, two children and stepdaughter as Choctaw Freedmen.

The Walton Enrollment Card[3]

Close examination of the enrollment card of the Walton Family reveals substantial information. The family members are clearly listed, Samuel, his wife Sallie, their son, Sam. Jr., another son Houston, and Samuel's stepdaughter Louisa. She was Sallie's daughter prior to their marriage.

---

[3] See Family enrollment card in Appendix section. The card is Choctaw Freedman Enrollment Card number 777

Note that on the card the fact that this was a Freedman enrollment is clearly inscribed at the top of the card. As Freedmen, their connection to a slave owner is indicated. Samuel, it points out was a slave of Jim Davis. Sallie was listed as a slave of Emeline Perry.

As stated earlier, when there is an opportunity to obtain further data from the files. On the bottom right hand side of the page, the date the family applied for enrollment was noted as June 29, 1899. The stamp on the left indicates that the family was approved for enrollment in 1904. In the years between 1899 and 1904, Louisa, Sallie's daughter had married.

On the enrollment card, a notation from the front of the card indicates that Louisa Ingram, now had children after the interview process had begun. The notation clearly tells the reader, "for information on the children of No. 5, (in this case Louisa) see N.B. #230.[4] This simply means that Choctaw Freedman New Born card #230 has more family data. Again, like the other records, there is an accompanying interview to be found in publication M1301. The file #230 of the Choctaw Freedman Newborns is where this will be found.

What resulted from pulling this file is another interview pertaining now to Sallie's grandchildren who were being enrolled by their father, George Sanders, who was now the husband to Louisa, Sallie's daughter. The interview was conducted in 1906, in Atoka, I.T. and the spokesperson for Louisa's children, was her husband, George Sanders.

The following is a transcription of that interview as it appears in the file.

---

[4] Ibid

From Choctaw Freedman
New Born Card No. 230
The Children of Louisa Ingram Sanders

DEPARTMENT OF THE INTERIOR
COMMISSIONER TO THE FIVE CIVILIZED TRIBES
CHOCTAW LAND OFFICE

Atoka, Indian Territory, December 31, 1906

In the matter of the application for the enrollment of John Henry, Ethel and Easter Sanders, as Choctaw Freedmen.

GEORGE SANDERS, being first duly sworn testified as follows:

Examination by the Commissioner.

Q. What is your name? A. George Sanders
Q. How old are you? A. Forty-four
Q. What is your Post Office address? A. Heavener, I.T.
Q. Are you a Choctaw freedman? A. No sir.
Q. You are a non-citizen? A. Yes sir.
Q. Do you appear here today for the purpose of giving testimony in the matter of the application for the enrollment of your three minor children, John Henry, Ethel and Easter Sanders? A. Yes Sir.
Q. Are these children all now living? A. Yes sir.
Q. Do they live with you? A. Yes, sir.
Q. What is the name of their mother? A. Louisa Sanders? She is enrolled as Louisa Ingram.
Q. Is she a Choctaw Freedman? A. Yes sir.
Q. Is she now living? A. yes sir.

95

Q. What is the name of the father of Louisa Sanders? A. Sam Walton.

Q. What is the name of her mother? We call her Kittie Walton.

Q. Was she ever called Sallie? A. Yes sir, we call her Kittie and Sallie and Sarah.

Q. Do you know what kin Houston and Sam Walton, Jr. are to your wife?

A. They say they are her brothers.

Q. Are they full brothers? A. Half brothers.

Q. Who is the father of Houston Walton? A. Sam Walton

Q. Who is the mother of Sam Walton? A. Well Kittie or Sallie, one I don't know which is her right name.

Q. Well how can Houston Walton and Sam Walton Jr. behalf brothers of your wife, when from your own testimony they appear to have the same father and mother? A. Well old man Sam raised her and she calls him Pa.

Q. Did you ever hear your wife refer to one John Williams?

Q. No sir.

Q. You are not positive that Samuel Walton is the father of your wife are you? A. No sir.

Q. Then you do not know who the father of your wife is?

A. No sir.

Louisa Sanders is identified on the approved roll of Choctaw freedmen as Louisa Ingram at No. 3751, and on Choctaw freedman field card No. 777, at No.5 thereon.

Q. There was received by the Commissioner to the Five Civilized Tribes on November 28, 1906, applications for the enrollment of John Henry, Ethel and Easter Sanders, as Choctaw freedmen, and the affidavits of Louisa Sanders, the mother of said John Henry, Ethel and Easter Sanders, and Sallie Walton, the mid-wife who was in attendance at the dates of the birth of said children, which affidavits were all duly signed and executed before R. L. Yandell, a notary public on the 26 day of November, 1906; were you present when these affidavits were signed and executed?

Q. Yes sir.

Q. Did you or your wife ever make application to the Commissioner for the enrollment of these three children prior to November 26, 1906? A. Yes sir, for Ethel.

Q. When and where did you make application for the enrolment of Ethel? A. At Hugo.

Q. When? A. February 18, 1905

Q. Before whom did you appear at that time to make application for the enrollment of Ethel Sanders as a Choctaw freedman?

Q. Mr. Yandell.

Q. Did your wife, Louisa Sanders, and Sallie Walton appear before him at that time? A. Yes sir.

Q. Did they sign and execute affidavits? A. Yes sir.

Q. What did you do with them? A. I carried them to the Post Office.

Q Where did you mail them to? Muskogee.

Q. Did you mail them to Muskogee immediately after their execution?

Q. Yes sir, the same day.

Q. You never made any other application or the enrollment of Easter and John Henry Sanders? A. No sir not any but this, on November 26, 1906.

Q. Then the applications you made for the enrollment of Easter and John Henry Sanders were the only applications you ever made for them? A. Yes sir.

Q. Have you any papers showing that you made application for the enrollment of Ethel Sanders on February 18, 1905? A. Yes sir.

The witness here offers in evidence certificates of R.L. Yandell, Sam Walton and Sallie Walton tending to show that application was made on February 18, 1905, for the enrollment of Ethel Sanders, which certificates are received and marked "Exhibits A, B, and C, and made a part of the record herein.

Witness Excused.

- - - - - - - - - - - - - - - - - - - -

I, Charles Bozarth, stenographer to the Commissioner to the Five Civilized Tribes, on oath state that the above is a full, true and correct transcript of my stenographic notes as taken in said cause on said date.

Charles Bozarth (his signature)

Subscribed and sworn to before me this 3 day of January 1907
W.F. Augell (his signature)

The interview that appeared above at first glance may not reveal much to the reader. However, being a part of the author's family, it was known among family members that Sallie, was often called *"Kittie"*. Here in this interview from her son-in-law, it is confirmed that this was a name of endearment used by the family towards her. The origin of the name "Kittie" was not known, for many years but the origin of the name was to come to light a few years later, through an old letter saved by one of Sallie's grandchildren. Kittie (or Kitty) was the name of Sallie's own grandmother. (See following letter.)

A Long Lost Letter

Sallie Walton, the wife of Samuel Walton, lived till 1961, when she died in Ft. Smith, Arkansas. There was not much information known about Sallie's life as a child, and virtually nothing about her parents. Samuel, her husband died in 1912, and Sallie did remarry. She married a man by the name of Harvey Lance. No children were born from this marriage and Sallie used the name Lance for only a brief time in her life. In 1923, Sallie was 60 years old and living in Arkansas. She wrote a letter to a friend living in Howe, Oklahoma, whose name was W.B. Billy inquiring about her own family. She received a response to that letter, addressed to her as Sallie "Lance" and she kept that letter until her death.

It was this letter that was located among the personal artifacts after Sallie's death, and then again in 1999, among the personal effects of Sallie's granddatughter Annie. Annie was one of the children mentioned in the testimony of George Sanders. Annie Easter Sanders was Sallie's granddaughter, and she died in 1999, in Maclester, Oklahoma. The letter was addressed to Sallie, The letter, because of the wonderful genealogical data is transcribed here, below.

Howe, Oklahoma
December 30, 1923

Dear Sallie Lance

Well, after so long, I will try your kind letter, in regard to your father and mother. Well, I did not no(sic) your father and mother myself, but I will write to you what Loman Jack told me to write, and tell you. Your grandmother's name is Kittie, and her husband's name was James Crow, and James Crow was full blood Indian, and Mandy Crow, she was daughty(sic) of Kitte and James Crow and Mandy was your mother. But Loman says he don't remember your father's name. But he rembers(sic) that you was just small child, when you mother married an Indian but name of Ochitubee. But Loman says that whether Ochitubee was your father or not, but may be just your step father, and so that's what Loman told me to write to you. In a way your grandfather James Crow was full blood Choctaw Indian and so Loman tol(sic) me to write and tell you about this and so this be all at this time. Were all well at this time and hope you are the same. I hope to hear from you soon.Am closing for this time. From your friend and a brother in Christ.

W.B. Billy
Howe, Oklahoma LeFora (sic)County

This letter is essential in learning more about the family history, particularly because it refers to Sallie's grandparents. It confirms that her mother was Amanda, who had married the Choctaw "Ochitubbe" as in the letter above. In the Dawes interview, Sallie refers to her mother as Amanda "Anchatubbe". Clearly, Amanda, is the same "Mandy" referred to in the letter, and the same Amanda whose name is in the family bible.

Many questions can be generated from reading this letter. Sallie was 60 years old in 1923. What was the situation that caused her to write to W.B. Billy inquiring about her parents and grandparents? Was she not raised with her mother or near her grandparents? Who was W.B. Billy in relation to the family to have such knowledge, and who was Loman Jack? The answers to these questions might not ever be known, but the value of the letter, telling Sallie the names of her grandparents, is one of those rare gems, that can only be found by sorting through old family papers, and memorabilia.

There were other documents in the collection of family memorabilia, including the Walton family bible that included the names of Sallie and her husband Samuel, and their children. However it is this letter that provided more pertinent genealogical data, taking the history of the family back to its earliest generations in Indian Territory.

Chapter 7

A Chickasaw Case Study
The Lewis Family - Chickasaw Freedmen

Chapter 7

A Chickasaw Case Study

The Lewis Family - Chickasaw Freedmen

One lesson learned from researching Freedmen records, is to note that all that is published pertaining to the Freedmen, is not all there is to the family history. The story of the Chickasaw Freedmen is a dramatic one where families were disenfranchised from the time the slaves were released from bondage, until Oklahoma statehood. These Freedmen often were related by blood to the very persons who disclaimed ties to them, and what appears in the Dawes records, is not always the entire story of the family. In both the Choctaw and Chickasaw Nations, the 41 years from 1866 to statehood in 1907, there was a constant struggle for the Freedmen to remain in the land of their birth, where they had toiled for decades. The effort was made to remove the Freedmen, once they were no longer useful to the nation as slaves, however, in so many cases the Freedmen had begun to organize themselves, to present their cases to Congress in an effort to ask for intervention on their behalf, and to also share in the benefits that were made to assist them.[1]

One of the leaders who worked continually for the Freedmen was a man known as Charles Cohee. This man was one of many of the officers of the Choctaw Chickasaw

---

[1] There was more than $300,000 that was agreed upon when the Treaty of 1866 was signed, that was to be used for the benefit of the Choctaw and Chickasaw Freedmen. There were many memorials and petitions to Congress made by the Freedmen and they often referred to this monetary assistance that they were to have received for schools, and other benefits to improve their lives in the Territory.

Freedmen's Association. There were over the years several organizations. By the time of the Dawes Commission, Charles Cohee, William Alexander, and others were among leaders in the Freedmen community who would speak on behalf of Freedmen applying for enrollment.

Brevity in Chickasaw Freedmen Interviews

In the case of many of the Chickasaw Freedmen application files, one will find short abbreviated statements, instead of detailed interviews. Were these shortened statements, the actual words made by the Chickasaw Freedmen? Probably not. Most Chickasaw Freedmen would have likely been more timid than assertive in the Dawes interview process, and they would not come in and simply make a statement and withdraw. So when one finds these small "statements" one is urged to dig deeper to see if there are additional documents reflecting the family's history. This point about the brevity of some of the interviews is emphasized, primarily because there are a number of records from Congressional records that indicate that there was great dissatisfaction with the outcome of the enrollment process. Subsequently, there were a good number of challenges made by Freedmen from both the Choctaw and Chickasaw nations, requesting transfer from the Freedmen rolls to the rolls by blood.

Many of those making challenges, initially had small-abbreviated interviews such as the one that will follow. In addition, there were also some efforts to prevent any changes to their status, when many had strong blood ties to the nations through their fathers. The family listed below is an example of some of the shortened files that one might find in many Chickasaw Dawes records.

.

The Family of Sarah Lewis

Sarah Lewis being sworn by commissioner A.S. McKennon says:

> *I am about 53 years old. I belonged to Sam Colbert.*
> *My unmarried children are Raford 18, Emily 16,*
> *and Caroline 13. My other children are: Ella, wife*
> *of John Albert, United States citizen. She has*
> *children Aaron Johnson 14, Samuel Johnson, 13,*
> *Ophelia Johnson 11, Daniel Albert, 6, Bertha Albert*
> *5, Helen Albert 3, and John Albert, 1. My daughter*
> *Lizzie was first wife of John Albert, by whom he had*
> *a child: Susan Albert. Maggie, the wife of James*
> *Carolina is a Creek. She is 26 years old. She has*
> *children: Bankston 7, Ed 3, and Frank 8 months.*
>
> *I went to Ft. Gibson, I went with Zack Kemp, Joe*
> *Nezer, Joe Kemp, and others. I remained there*
> *about a year. I went in the same year that peace was*
> *made. I came back in the fall. It was pleasant*
> *weather.*

In the same file of Sarah Lewis, one finds a statement from Charles Cohee. However, instead of his exact testimony, there appears to be a summary of what he stated.

> *Charles Cohee states that he went down to Sam*
> *Colbert's on Red River in September 1865, and that*
> *this was about 3 weeks before Sarah Lewis and*
> *others left for Fort Gibson, and that the heard of*
> *them leaving after he got back home. He knows this*
> *because his father Frazier McLish, Ed Colbert had*
> *gone down to where they were making the treaty at*
> *Fort Smith. They had gone to Fort Smith before he*
> *went down to Colbert's.*

Sarah Lewis
Radford Lewis
Emily Lewis
Caroline Lewis
 enrolled.

One can note from this file that only the younger children of Sarah Lewis were included when she enrolled. Since her other children were older and married, they were not admitted to the tribal rolls with her. They would have to apply separately for enrollment. But like many of the Chickasaw records, these were brief summaries recorded, although by their content, one can definitely note that a full interview did still take place.

The presence of Charles Cohee being interviewed is just as interesting, particularly because he had been a dynamic leader in the Chickasaw Nation. He also clearly had a relationship to Sarah Lewis and they were tied to each other through the Colbert line. The simple fact that the interview is included in the Lewis family file should tell the researcher that there is a relationship between the two households of Chickasaw Freedmen. In addition, he refers to the time when the Treaty of 1866 was being signed in 1866 and the fact that they were present throughout the decades, in the Territory.

It should also be noted that this enrollment process for Chickasaw Freedmen yielded very little in terms of monetary gain or in some cases much land access. It should be noted that Chickasaw Freedmen were never officially adopted by their nation, although they remained by the thousands in the land of their birth, and retained much of the culture and customs of their nation.

Chapter 8

A Seminole Case Study
The Case of Samuel Mahardy

Chapter 8

A Seminole Case Study
The Case of Samuel Maharby

The records from the Seminole Nation are interesting to utilize, particularly for the unique history from which they emerge. The Seminoles, who were a combination of blended peoples who were remaining persons coming from the Red Stick factions of the Muscogee people. In addition, after entering Florida, they mixed with the Africans who had fled bondage from the Carolinas and Georgia. Both groups joined their efforts and formed a united front against a common enemy. This is important to understand when reading the cases. The Seminoles were mixed with Africans and with Creeks, from whom they had separated, and when in Indian Territory, they also had relationships with people from other tribes, as well.

It is important to note that the actual Seminole nation was small, and that the number of Freedmen in that nation was even smaller. In these records one will find death certificates, letters, and some testimonies. The records will be mixed in some cases of the Seminoles, both by blood and Freedmen and many of the Seminole Freedmen files are also empty.

Again the unique history of the Seminoles and their initial rejection of the concept of slavery must be emphasized in order to understand how so many of the records of the Freedmen and their fellow Seminoles by blood are filed together. The Seminoles did purchase slaves when they arrived in Indian Territory but these were Africans who had already lived among them before removal. Some arrived as free people, with free papers, but upon arrival in the Territory there was immediate threat of slave hunters some from white slave traders, and some from the former enemy of the old Red Sticks, the Creek Nation.

The case of Seminole Freedmen #236 deserves to be examined because of the wealth of information revealed in the testimony. Samuel Mahardy was born in the Seminole Nation of a Chickasaw father. Samuel wanted to identify with his father's culture of the Chickasaw, and as a young adult, he sought enrollment by blood in that Nation. Several examinations were required to hear this case, and what unfolds is an enlightening look at the life and culture of the Indian and Africans who lived side by side in the Seminole Nation. The first interview in the file was with Samuel's mother Betsey Mahardy, a woman uncertain of her age. She was born a slave, yet she was free to marry and travel and as the testimony reveals, she had close family members who were not slaves at all. This information is significant for any student of Seminole and African American history.

Betsey Mahardy, being duly sworn, testified as follows:

Commissioner:
Q.   What is your name?
A.   Betsey Mahardy.
Q.   How old are you?
A.   I can't say just how old I am for I can't keep account
      of it
A.   Where do you live?
A.   In the Chickasaw Nation.
Q.   What is your post office address?
A.   Davis
Q.   Are you a citizen of the Chickasaw Nation.
A.   No sir.

Q. Of what nation are you a citizen?
A. I am Creek. During the war I went out with the ones that went to the Seminole Nation and I didn't go with the ones that come back this way.
Q. Didn't you belong to a Seminole Indian?
A. No sir no Seminole Indian ever owned me.
Q. Haven't you enrollment in the Seminole Nation?
A. Yes sir, my folks done it unbeknownst to me.
Q. Haven't you received an allotment in the Seminole Nation?
A. No sir, I don't know anything about it. I never have seen my land.
Q. Have you ever been enrolled in any other Nation than the Seminole?
A. No sir, they enrolled me on there.

The name of the witness appears upon the final roll of the citizens of the Seminole nation, approved by the Secretary of the Interior on April 2, 1901, opposite No. 2739 as Betsey Mahardy, 57 years of age, and having been identified as a citizen of the Seminole Nation and a member of the Caesar Bruner Freedman Band. An allotment of the lands for the Seminole nation was made to Betsey Mahardy in the year 1901.

By Mr. Apple:
Q. Did you ever make any application at the land office for any land?
A. No sir.
Q. You never made formal application for the allotment that was made to you in the Seminole Nation?
A. No sir.
Q. Did you ever apply to the Dawes Commission for enrollment as a Seminole by blood or as a freedman?
A. No sir, my folks done it unknownst (sic) to me.
Q. Who of your folks do you refer to?

A.   Ben Bruner's wife. She is a widow now.

Q.   Is she a freedman or a Seminole?

A.   Seminole.

Q.   How was she related to you?

A.   She was my sister.

Q.   Is she living now?

A.   I don't know. I haven't heard from her in a long time.

Q.   Did you authorize her as your agent to make application for that land for you?

A.   No sir, I never have.

Q.   You are the mother of the application Samuel Mahardy?

A.   Yes sir.

Q.   Who was his father?

A.   Wyatt Mahardy.

Q.   When were you married to Wyatt Mahardy?

A.   I couldn't tell you when I was married to him.

Q.   Fix the date as early as you can.

A.   I don't know about the date. I don't know the date of nothing. I never went to school, and never paid no attention to nothing like that.

Q.   Were you a slave before the war?

A.   Yes sir.

Q.   Were you married to Wyatt Mahardy before or after the Civil War.

A.   Before-no, during the war.

Q.   Was the war going on?

A.   Yes sir.

Q.   You said you made flight from the Creek country down south?

A.   Yes sir, from the Creek country to the Seminole country.

Q.   Had you been married before that time?

A.   No sir.

Q.   Were you in the Seminole country when you married Wyatt Mahardy?

A. No we had gone to the Chickasaw nation.
Q. How long had you been in the Chickasaw nation when you married Wyatt Mahardy?
A. Two years.
Q. Are you positive that the war was still going on when you married him?
A. Yes sir.
Q. Do you know when the soldiers returned from the war?
A. No sir, I don't.
Q. Did you and Wyatt Mahardy have any other child older than Sam?
A. No sir.
Q. You did have one didn't you?
A. Yes sir, older than Sam.
Q. Had you been married once before you married Wyatt?
A. Yes sir.
Q. Did you understand me a while ago when I asked you if you had ever been married before?
A. No I didn't understand.
Q. Who was your first husband?
A. Bruner.
Q. Where were you living when you were married to him?
A. In the Creek Nation.
Q. Was it before or after the war?
A. Before
Q. Did you have any children by Bruner?
A. Yes sir, one.
Q. What is his name?
A. Richard Bruner.
Q. Is he living?
A. Yes, sir.
Q. Is he enrolled?
A. On the Seminole Roll.

Q.	Does he live in the Seminole Nation?
A.	No he lives in the Chickasaw Nation.
Q.	Do you know the date of Sam's birth?
A.	No I don't.
Q.	Do you know under what law you were married to Wyatt?
A.	Chickasaw.
Q.	Did he have a Chickasaw license?
A.	Yes sir, he did.
Q.	Have you that license now?
A.	No we didn't have no license.
Q.	Who married you?
A.	John Ishtone, a full blood.
Q.	Was he a preacher or a judge?
A.	He was a full blood but he married white folks, Indians and colored folks.
Q.	Was John Ishtone a full blood Chickasaw Indian?
A.	Yes sir.
Q.	Did he give you a certificate?
A.	No sir.
Q.	Never gave any papers of any sort?
A.	No sir.
Q.	Where were you living at the time you were married?
A.	In the Chickasaw Nation.
Q.	Where were you at the time you married-were you at your home, or a church or where?
A.	John Ishtone's home.
Q.	Where did he live?
A.	On Rock Creek.
Q.	What direction did he live from the present town of Davis?
A.	I don't know. I know it was on Rock Creek.
Q.	What direction is that from where you lived?
A.	Toward Mill Creek.
Q.	South of you.
A.	No, east.

Q. Did you continue to reside in the Chickasaw Nation?
A. Yes sir.
Q. You have never lived anywhere else?
A. No sir.
Commissioner:
Q. You said that at the time the Civil War began you were living in the Creek Nation?
A. No sir, I had done come to the Seminole nation, and when I was ready to go back the war had broke out.
Q. Where were you living when the war began?
A. In the Seminole.
Q. Weren't you a slave at the time the war began?
A. Yes sir.
Q. Who did you belong to?
A. The Bruner.
Q. What Bruner?
A. I don't know what Bruner-Ryder Bruner was his name
Q. What Nation was he a citizen of ?
A. Creek.
Q. When were you freed?
A. What do you mean by that?
Q. Were you a slave to Bruner all during the war?
A. Yes sir, till they set them all free.
Q. Till the slaves were emancipated?
A. Yes sir.
Q. Now you said your first husband was a man named Bruner. Was he a slave?
A. No sir.
Q. Was you ever married to Bruner, or did he just live with you?
A. Yes sir, I was married to him, he was an Indian.
Q. What do you mean by saying that you were a slavc, and yet was married to this Indian?
A. Indians has slaves.

Q. You said you were married to Bruner who was an Indian. Are you sure you were married to him?
A. I married him.
Q. You had one child by Bruner?
A. Yes sir.
Q. What was his name?
A. Richard Bruner.
Q. Is Richard living now?
A. Yes sir.
Q. How old a man is Richard?
A. He is 45.
Q. How old was Richard when you married Wyatt Mahardy?
A. Three years old.

The interview with Betsey Mahardy continued with additional questions about her marriage to the Indian while she was a slave. The purpose of the interview initially was to place her son Samuel in the Chickasaw Nation since his father was a Chickasaw by blood. A Chickasaw followed Betsey Mahardy's interview who testified for them and eventually Samuel Mahardy who testified himself. He was examined and cross-examined by the Commission even more thoroughly than his mother. The final outcome of the interview was that Samuel Mahardy's application for enrollment with the Chickasaw nation as a citizen by blood was denied, in spite of the fact that his father was a Chickasaw Indian. As a result his file remained in the Seminole Nation. [1]

---

[1] This case is an interesting one, as it reflects a unique closeness between Seminole communities, and the lesser degree of closeness in Chickasaw communities, even among those with blood ties. Those with Seminole ancestry are encouraged to use the records designated both "by blood" and "Freedmen". The families were often intermingled and their relationships were strong.

Chapter 9

Exploring the Culture & Lifestyle
Of Black Indian Ancestors

Chapter 9

Exploring the Culture & Lifestyle of the Oklahoma Freedmen

"The best words are the words of the Black Indians themselves."

Genealogical research is a research process that crosses many disciplines. History, geography, sociology, preservation, law, cartography, and much more can be integral parts of the family history research process. The thorough researcher wants to go beyond a collection of names as one's genealogy unfolds. The researcher wants to gain an understanding of the culture and historical circumstances that shaped the lives of the ancestors. Black Indian research therefore should be no different.

Very often there is a temptation to merely settle for some documentation of the fact that there may have been a particular racial mixture in one's family line. However to settle for this as giving substance to one's genealogical research, is to leave the knowledge of this historical and cultural roots of the family, with gaping holes.

How then does the African-Native American genealogist find those pieces of family history that reveal more of culture and lifestyle lived by one's ancestors? Where does one go to find the remaining information that will add to the breadth of knowledge about those in pre-statehood Indian Territory?

The scholar will find that the best source of much data comes from those who lived the lives being studied. In other words, critical information about the lives of the Oklahoma black Indians, come from the stories they told, and the answers to questions they made. The words of the black Indians themselves reveal some of the richest data about their culture. Two sources are recommended as a beginning source. These are the **Indian Pioneer Papers**, and the **WPA Slave Narratives.**

The Oklahoma Indian Pioneer papers housed at the University of Oklahoma, and at the Oklahoma Historical Society reveal in more than 100 volumes interviews reflecting the lives of early citizens, white, black and red. This was part of an oral history initiative that was paralleled the Federal Writers project. Thousands of oral histories were collected in the same time period of the WPA project, in the late 1930s. From these interviews come remarkable sources of information about the lifestyle and culture of the people. Included in these interviews were also Freedmen interviews.

This interview of Island Smith, a Creek Freedman provides a significant insight into his life and how he lived.[1]

Indian Pioneer Papers ----
Island Smith, Creek Freedman

I am on the Creek rolls as a part Creek. My father was a Negro, and my mother one-half Creek and one half Negro.[2]

---

[1] Indian Pioneer Papers, Interview with Island Smith Volume 85, Interview #6729 on July 17, 1937.

[2] Island Smith's mother is identified on the interview as Hannah Robinson. She was still alive at the time of the interview in 1937, and Smith shared with the interviewer that his mother was 12 years old "when the stars fell." This is a reference to the Leonid Meteor Shower of 1833 that was seen over most of North America. She may have been one of the longest living Freedmen.

I am a member of Canadian colored town. Pearo Bruner was the Town King.[3] Our symbol was a bear. Salle Morner was my aunt and Yahola Harjo was my uncle.

Schooling
I never attended any schools in the Creek Nation. There weren't any here when I was a boy. When they were established, I was too old to attend.

Farming
My parents raised only about an acre of corn every year. They raised some cattle and hogs, which just ran wild. My father had also about 150 head of horses. I only have one Indian pony left. The others have all died. He stands about four feet high and is 3 years old.

Game
We killed all manner of game native to the Creek Nation. We had pet deer, coon, possums, turkeys, rattlesnakes and wolf-dogs. The wolfdogs would get to be fairly gentle, but would leave if strangers came round. We never killed rattlesnakes as it was a violation of the law. Offenders were given 50 lashes on the bar back, if convicted.

We never raised any chickens, turkeys, or guineas until the 90's or until the wild fowl began to be thinned out. I have guineas now that I believe to still have a strain of prairie chicken in them.

---

[3] The name of the town king is most often printed as Paro Bruner.

U.S. Marshals
Bas Reed [4], Crowder Nicks, Lee and Colbert were some of the marshals I remember. Jesse Allen, who is still living, was a deputy, also.

Cherokee Bill
My mother nursed Cherokee Bill. His mother was white and his father Cherokee Indian.[5]

I used to fiddle for dances, with a violin, which was owned by Cherokee Bill and on which he carved his initials. I was offered $150 for it, but refused to part with it. It became warped one time and I left it in Okfuskee to be repaired. The jeweler with whom I left it said it was stolen from his shop.

Almanac
When I was a boy, we didn't receive calendars from the traders as people do form stores today. A man would come around and sell an almanac for fifty cents. He usually sold one every third or fourth house. If we didn't happen to purchase one, we would sometimes have to go see our neighbor to find out the day of the month.

Food
We prepared Sofkey and Puskee from the corn we raised. If fact, I still make Puskee.

---

[4] Although written as Reed, Smith is referring to Bass Reeves, US Deputy Marshal who worked in the Western District Court for Judge Isaac C. Parker.

[5] This reference to Cherokee Bill's parentage is actually in error. Crawford Goldsby, was Cherokee Bill's real name and his mother was a Cherokee Freedwoman Ellen Lynch, and his father was George Goldsby, a fair skinned black man who served with the U.S. Colored Troops in the Civil War.

We used to trade hogs for flour, which was shipped in from Texas and Arkansas. Two year-old hogs sold for $1.50 each.

Grapes, berries, pecans, hickory and walnuts were gathered from the woods and were an important addition to our food supply.

Medicine
When we got the chills in the winter, we would break the ice if need be, and jump into the water. This would break the chills.

Certain roots, herbs and barks were used by the Creeks as medicine, I have learned about a lot of this and doctor people for various disorders. I know them when I see them and what they are used for. After a funeral, people would gather or buy some Mecoo-Anesia (Kingroot) and wash in it so they wouldn't get sick.

Marriage
When I got married, people never used a ceremony. I asked the woman if she would be my wife. When she said yes, we considered ourselves married.

It cost me $65, and $75, the second time I was married, for food to prepare a feast for friends and relatives.

This interview with Island Smith revealed how much he knew about history and life in the Territory. He spoke about the Trading posts, the Green Peach war, and other aspects of life, including the traditional ball games, often played in the Territory between tribal towns.

I remember attending at least two of the Indian ball games held at Nuyaka. One of them was between Nuyaka and Hilaby Towns. This game ran into a big fight and one man was killed and several badly injured before it could be stopped. Ben Grayson of Hilaby town was the medicine makers. I don't remember the year this happened, but it was in the Territory days.

The Green Peach War
The government sent about 1800 troops to quall the uprising caused by Esparhecher. They came through Okmulgee and camped out here on a creek. We tired to talk to them, but they wouldn't talk. They were little black men, not much bigger than I was, who wore uniforms with brass buttons. They were riding small horses and carried .38-40 Colt pistols. The wagons, which had iron wheels and spokes, were drawn by big mules. Small flags were attached to the bridles of these teams.

My uncle, Morris Rentie and a neighbor names Frazier Robinson were with the warriors out in the Sac and Fox reservation.

The interview with Island Smith is so valuable, even with some of the names misspoken, or misreported, it is clear that Smith was still a witness to many things that took place in 19th century Indian Territory.

Slave Narratives, Another Valuable Source

As valuable as the Indian Pioneer Interviews are, the WPA Slave Narratives, part of the Federal Writers Project also provides an interesting glimpse into the life of those enslaved by the tribes of Oklahoma. They provide a wealth

124

of data about the lifestyle in Indian Territory. From them one learns about diet, cooking methods, burial traditions, dress, and more.

Traditional Food

"We cooked all sorts of Indian dishes: Tom-fuller, pashofa, hickory-nut grot, Tom-budha, ash-cakes, and pound cakes besides vegetables and mat dishes. Corn or corn meal was used in all de Indian dishes. We made hominy out'n de whole grains. Tom-fuller was made from beaten corn and tasted sort of like hominy."

"We would take corn and beat it like in a wooden mortar wid a wooden pestle. We would husk it by fanning it and we would den put in on to cook in a big pot. While it was cooking we'd pick out a lot of hickory-nuts, tie' em up in a cloth and beat'em a little and drop 'em in and cook for a long time. We called dis dish hickory-nut grot. When we made pashofa we beat de corn and cook for a little while and den we add fresh pork and cook until de meat was done. Tom-budha was green corn and fresh meat cooked together and seasoned wid' tongue or pepper-grass."[6]
-Polly Colbert-

Creek Burial Customs
....The Creek sho take on when somebody die!

---

[6] This interview was with Polly Colbert of the Choctaw Nation. She was interviewed in 1937, and described much in detail of the methods of preparing traditional Indian dishes.

Long in de night you wake up and hear a gun go off, way yonder somewhar. Den it go again and again, jest as fast as they can ram de load in. Dat mean somebody die. When somebody die, de men go out in de yard and let people know dat way. Den dey jest go back in de house and let de fire go out and don't even tech de dead person till somebody get dar who has a right to touch de dead.

When somebody had sick dey build a fire in de house, even in de summer and don't let it die down till dat person git well or die. When dey die dey lit de fire out.

In de morning everybody dress up fine and go to de house whar de dead is and stand around in de yard outside de house and don't go in. Pretty soon along come somebody what got a right to tech and handle de dead and dey go in. I don't know what give dem de right, but I thinking dey has to go through some kind of medicine to get de right, and I know dey has to drink de red root and purge good before day tech de body.[7]
-Lucinda Davis-

Occasionally, one discovers some additional resources from unpublished data. In 1933, an Oklahoma scholar, Samuel Sameth wrote his doctoral dissertation on the culture of the Creek Freedmen. Entitled, *Creek Negroes,*

---

[7] This excerpt from the narrative of Lucinda Davis is said to be one of the best interviews of life in Indian Territory that emerged from the Slave Narrative process. Lucinda, fluent in Muskogee Creek language, and a child during the Civil War was one of the few people who could tell about the famous battle of Honey Springs from the civilian perspective, having been an eyewitness. In addition, she also revealed many customs having still been one who practiced them till the time of her death.

A Study of Race Relations, he interviewed a large number of Black Creek Citizens who spoke of their lifestyle. They also shared with him their perspective about the relationship between Creek Freedmen and State Negroes who had recently become a large part of the Oklahoma population. Some of these insights into life among the Creek Negroes are fascinating to read.[8]

Burial Grounds

One very significant interview from the Indian Pioneer Papers give a bit of history on the Old Agency Cemetery, perhaps the most historically significant burial grounds in Indian Territory.

Burials at this cemetery began at least four decades before statehood. Lying at the foot of Agency Hill, this cemetery, now abandoned, holds the burial sites of some of the most important leaders from both the Creek Nation, and Indian Territory history. There are hundreds of Creeks buried in this   10 acre burial ground, some buried in traditional graves, others with standard military markers and others with magnificent marble monuments. Some of the noted leaders entered there have remarkable six-foot marble markers while others, in contrast were humble hand carved field stones with the names chiseled into slates of rock.

There are many other Black Indian burial sites that also remain in Oklahoma, such as the Durant Family Cemetery not far from Old Agency, Four Mile Branch Church Cemetery in Ft. Gibson, and Cane Creek Cemetery in Boynton. However, Old Agency is probably the largest

---

[8] Sameth's dissertation can be found at the University of Oklahoma, Norman. Though never published, it revealed much detail regarding cultural identity of Freedmen, as well as practiced customs, and the relations between state Negroes and native Creek Freedmen.

Black Indian Cemetery known to exist and it holds of the remainder of several African Town Kings, former tribal council members, and leaders from the House of Warriors and the House of Kings. Sugar T. George, Harry Island, and Peter Stidham are among the Creek leaders buried in this burial ground. Though much neglected, there is now an effort being led by a community activist in the Muskogee area to save this important burial ground. The first historical reference to Old Agency cemetery was made in the 1930s in the Indian Pioneer interviews and James Buchannan made several of the inscriptions.

Like all aspects of genealogy, an interest in the preservation of the cemeteries where Oklahoma's Black Indian population lies buried is essential. There are many efforts underway to preserve cemeteries in Oklahoma, and hopefully the many descendants of Oklahoma Freedmen will join this critical effort.[9]

Through careful examination of sources such as the Pioneer papers, slave narratives, and countless other interviews, the researcher will quickly discover that the best discovery of this missing history will be found in the words of the Black Indians, themselves.

---

[9] Sue Tolbert of Muskogee Oklahoma is spearheading a movement to preserve Oklahoma Cemeteries, and Old Agency Cemetery has been a major effort of hers. She initiated the first cleanup of the cemetery in spring 2005, and plans to continue with the restoration of this important burial site.

Chapter 10

Beyond Oklahoma
Eastern Tribes & Tri-Racial
Ancestors

Chapter 10

Beyond Oklahoma
Eastern Tribes and Tri-Racial Ancestors

It should be stated that the Five Nations of Oklahoma are not the only tribes where one will find mixed people. One reason is that the southeastern tribes were not the only tribes affected by the institution of slavery. From the earliest days of the arrival of Europeans in the Americas, efforts were made to enslave the indigenous people right away. In addition, some of the Algonquin tribes of New England also had early exposure to Africans and some had produced offspring, dating from the existence of slavery in the northern states. [1]

Among some of the tribes known to have had contact with early African both slaves and free, were the Wampanoag, Narrangassett, Pequot, Paugausset, Shinnecock, Montauk, Nanticoke, and others. In addition, several tribes of the Powhatan confederacy of Virginia, including the Pamunkey, and Mattaponi also had early exposure that resulted in blended families.

Scholar Frederick Hodge noted at the beginning of the 20th century that in some of the tribes, the mixture with back was so complete that "the Indian blood has been so

---

[1] Hodge, Frederick Webb, ed. Handbook of American Indians North of Mexico. Bureau of American Ethnology, Belltin 30. Washington DC: U.S. Government Printing Office, 1907, 2 vols.

mingled with that of the Negro that all trace of the original Narragansett has vanished." [2]

In recent years the Mashantucket Pequots gained federal recognition. They are a small tribe in Connecticut who gained much national attention afterwards. Part of the attention stemmed from their having opened the now famous Foxwood Casino. The second reason for their fame is the composition of the tribe. To many who are outside of the Pequot tribe, the members are black. However, in spite of the African ancestored appearance of many in the tribe, this small tribe kept its history among its members, as well as papers pertaining to the original treaties, and qualified in every way for Federal recognition. The Mashantucket Pequot nation has thrived in the short term since Federal recognition. They are among several people from the northeast that mixed with persons of African descent.

Expanding the Genealogical Search

It is not unusual to find that in spite of the many records from Indian Territory that can be found, at some time one's research will require that one look beyond Oklahoma to other documents from other states. It will also require learning the history of those eastern states, and becoming familiar with other kinds of records. In addition, the family may have had mixed ancestors, Indian, black, and white, so the sooner one learns how to negotiate those records, the sooner the research can continue. The "Black Indian" researcher should not be surprised to learn that there may be some white ancestry in the family as well. Acknowledging the possibility of having a tri-racial background can eventually take the researcher down another path to a new

---

[2] Hodge, op. cit. Vol II p. 51-53

level of documents for research. One should become familiar with the additional records, in order to continue the search.

There can be a blood tie that African-Native people have to a number of eastern tribes and it will enhance one's research to become familiar with them. Several are listed below:

Records Relating to the Enrollment of the Eastern Cherokee - The Guion Miller rolls 1908-1910 --M685

This record includes reports by Guion Miller and the actual roll of the Eastern Cherokee. Miller used a number of resources to compile this data including the Drennan Roll, the Hester Roll, and the Old Settler rolls. This set of records is listed at the National Archives as publication *M685*

Indian Census rolls 1885-1940 -- M692

There are hundreds of miscellaneous rolls of Indian data taken throughout the country throughout a number of years. More than 695 reels of microfilm pertaining to these records, are in this group, some from Indian schools, others from various tribes both east and west. As late as 1930 the rolls show degree of Indian blood, marital status, residence and other data. It should be noted that the records of the Blackfeet are not those of any tribes in the east, but of the Blackfeet located in Browning, Montana.[3]

---

[3] The Blackfeet are often misstated as being part of mixed families in the southeast United States. There have never been any tribal rolls or treaties signed with any indigenous people in the southeastern states called Blackfeet,(or Blackfoot) from that part of the country. There are no records reflecting removal of indigenous people by that designation to other states. There are some who state that the claim of being Blackfoot is a name applied to some who may have descended from Saponi Indians. However, no record set exists reflecting a tribe by the Blackfoot name.

Microfilm Publication M692

Some of the records to look at are:

> **Carlisle School -Reel 22**
> **Cherokee North Carolina - Reels 22-26**
> **Choctaw Mississippi reel 40**
> **Seminole (Florida) Reels 486-487**

Microfilm Publication M 348
The Eastern Cherokee & Eastern Cherokee Claims

The US Court of Claims was established in 1855 to hear claims against the United States. In 1905, the court ruled in favor of the Eastern Cherokee and required that all persons be identified who were entitled to participate in the distribution of payment of claims. More than $1 million was set aside for the payment of claims. Guion Miller a special agent on the Department of the Interior compiled a roll of all Eastern and Western Cherokee Indians who could establish that they were alive during the time of the treaties, or were descendants of persons who were. What remains is a wealth of data for researchers.

It should not be assumed that if one's ancestor had another tribal affiliation that they were not among the applicants. There were literally thousands of applicants who made claims, some who were in the tribe, and others who were not. Many were rejected, however, the data that remains from these applications is still there. It is recommended that therefore one use these records both among those who were accepted and those who were not. In many cases, some families were rejected because there was African blood in the family line, not because of an absence of Cherokee blood. To understand the biases of the roll will assist one to freely look at all aspects of the documents closely.

Tri-Racial Ancestors

One of the most valuable pieces of genealogical research about Africans and Indians outside of Indian Territory has emerged from the work of Dr. Virginia Easley DeMarce. In 1992, the *National Genealogical Society Quarterly* published her work on what she called the "Tri-Racial Isolates" in the Upper South. The Upper South consisting of Virginia, the Carolinas, Kentucky and Tennessee, her article is essential for any researcher whose ancestors may have been of mixed ancestry.[4]

The work is essential because Dr. DeMarce closely identifies and examines the migration patterns of these groups. By understanding the tri-racial population that individuals may be able to penetrate the realm of possibility of Indian ancestry. Her work is mentioned, because of the thousands of African Americans from Virginia to the Carolinas who claim Native American Ancestry, but who have no direction as to where to go to document this relationship. The effort to trace Indian ancestry from the Upper South is probably on one of the more challenging areas of Black-Indian Genealogy.

For persons with ancestors from the Upper South, there are distinct challenges because there was a deliberated effort to eliminate other tribes, especially the smaller tribe, by simply eliminating them from the census. It was not uncommon to learn that many tribes were simply

---

[4] DeMarce, Virginia Easley, *Verry SlightlyMixt: Tri-Racial Isolate Families of the Upper South. A Genealogical Study* National Genealogical Society Quarterly, March 1992 p. 5-35.

"terminated" by act of elimination of their racial category on the Federal census and other records. This official "termination" gave the impression that the population in some communities, were either black or white, and that the indigenous populations had become extinct. This later became more complicated when there was some complicity in this process. Some of the individuals who were of mixed ancestry, willingly accepted a designation as "white" which would provide them with greater access to more privileges in 19th century America.

Marriages and Migration Patterns

Relations between blacks and Indians have known to occur as far back as the 1600's. African and Indian marriages did occur, but this was neither a trend nor a widespread phenomena. However, there were some nations that did establish a pattern of intermarrying with both blacks and whites. For example, on the Eastern Shore of Virginia, DeMarce points out that the Gingaskins were intermarrying into both the black and white communities. And both whites and blacks are known to have married into the Nottoway, according to the census of 1808. Tribal trustees, who had first-hand knowledge of the composition of their tribe, made the particular census.

Note that the black participants in legally recognized marriages were primarily free blacks, who had some freedom to intermarry. After the Civil War, intermarrying continued, even though in many places it was still illegal. But when intermarrying occurred, there appeared to be a pattern of selectivity among bi-racial offspring, who usually selected a spouse from other bi-racial groups. This marriage pattern led to many bi-racial family structures becoming tri-racial.[5]

As the members of these mixed families sought to find marriage partners there was often a more frequent incidence of movement among some of these families than of non-mixed families in the general population.[6] In other words, the mixed families were seeking other families that were at least mixed, if not marrying into white families. This pattern comes as no surprise, to black family researchers, as it has not been usually to note that many mulattoes, or light skinned persons have for generations practiced the pattern of marrying exclusively other light skinned persons.

Tri-Racial Groups

Certain nicknames are given to describe tri-racial groups and these labels are used today throughout parts of the south. Labels such as *Brass Ankles, Red Bones, Lumbees,* and *Turks* are among the common names often used to describe tri-racial people. There are other names such as the *Guineas*, the *Haliwas* and the *Melungeons* or *Goins*. The families in those groups were bi-racial, or tri-racial and married as a general rule with other known mixed families. For example with the **Goins** clan, which is a long standing tri-racial family from Tennessee, they were known to have lived with and intermarried frequently with other groups such as the *Red Bones*, of Louisiana.[7]

---

[5] It was noted how the change occurred, when Indian/White, Indian /Black or White/Black offspring started intermarrying among themselves, thus creating tri-racial families.

[6] DeMarce points out this with the example of the Baltrip, or Boltrip family. This family is commonly found in the central part of North Carolina at one time, and then later appears as a free colored family in Wilkens County, farther to the west.

There have been many mixtures between Indians and whites and Indians and blacks over three centuries. However, there were no towns where exclusively these mixed people dominated. They became small pockets of people in the minority living in a larger European dominated culture. The merger of these cultures contributed to the loss of Indian languages and traditions. As a result most of the tri-racial families were either black-identified or white-identified families although genetically and historically they are tri-racial.

Notes on Searching for Tri-Racial ancestors.

Virginia DeMarce does make the effort to identify certain surnames of specific groups. For example, the Louisiana Red Bones frequently have the surname of *Willis, Sweat, Ashworth, or Perkins*. Scholar Gary Mills has also done a similar study on naming patterns of the mixed people who were free people of color in Louisiana.[8]

It will be helpful to become acquainted with the surnames from these groups, but the challenge exists in identifying Indian ancestors. Fortunately there are some leads that may assist the researcher in this effort. The researcher is cautioned that this quest will be extremely challenging since the extensive documentation just doesn't exist for tri-racial groups.

---

[7] The surname Goins is a variation of the group name Melungeons or Melongoins.

[8] Mills, Gary B. *Tracing Free Peple of Color in the Antebellum South*. The National Genealogy Society Quarterly, December, 1990. In this work, Mills discusses the origin of some families such as the Goins, Chavis, Locklear, Hunt, Ivey, Kennedy, Scott and Sampson families. Some of these names were also those of free non-whites in Alabama.

If one has the benefit of an oral tradition in the family that gives the name of an Indian ancestor, then one has already moved ahead a few steps I the research. However, care should be taken that the much sought for "Indian" ancestor is truly the Indian, and not another mixed person of color. With many persons of mixed heritage, the "full blood" Indian ancestor might actually be a more distant ancestor than the one that oral tradition may indicate.

This pursuit is largely dependent upon one learning the history, geography and demographics of the region. If there was an Indian tribe that lived in the region of one's ancestors one will have to learn the history of that specific tribe, become familiar with the names found in that group and then relate the history of their family to the history of that group.

There is a possible pitfall at this state for the genealogist. The search for Indian ancestors from the tri-racial perspective might steer the researcher into a frantic search to prove or disprove a specific racial composition. It is essential to keep the focus on the search for the names of those ancestors, regardless of their racial composition.

Virginia DeMarce herself acknowledged that her research could not have been published in the 1970s or even 1980s. This is because so many would not have wanted their mixed ancestry to be known, preferring to blend into the white population. Likewise, there are many African ancestored researchers who would not want to have to acknowledge a black/white mixture in their families, and who will prefer to search for the often mentioned Indian in the family line, also. In some cases the primary motivation was to blend into the majority population as quickly as possible. This is similar to immigrant populations who discourage children from speaking the mother tongue, with the intention to blend with the majority more easily.

There are two important tasks for the tri-racial family researcher. First one must learn as many of the surnames that have occurred in the family's history. Secondly one must learn as many of the surnames that appear among the different groups. Since there are groups such as the Red Bones, or Melungeons in several states, one may choose to become familiar with as many of the families of the same group in other areas.

Tribes Contributing to the Tri-Racial Groups

Members of some of the larger established Indian tribes married into the African race, but tribes such as the Catawba are not considered to be tri-racial as a tribe. There are other nations among whom many black Americans can claim ancestry. It is not unusual to hear many blacks of coastal states referring frequently to Pamunkey ancestors and to hear references to other groups such as the Lumbees.[9]

In the case of researching ancestors from the areas of North and South Carolina and other communities where tri-racial people lived, traditional census records will be essential in the research, and careful notation should be noted when one encounters the mulatto ancestor, who may

---

[9] The Lumbee Indians are still seeking official tribal recognition. This is challenged by the fact that the earliest European contact with the group known as the Lumbees, found them to be an English-speaking groups with customs and lifestyles of the European settlers. In addition there was no traditional "land mass" attributed to the Lumbees as a tribe. DeMarce notes that the Haliwas are an "artificial" Indian group with the name deriving from the beginning syllables of Halifax and Warren counties.

indeed have been part Indian from one of the woodlands tribes.

At the same time, the *Blackfoot* factor appears again in the quest for the Indian ancestor. Close scrutiny of the records will point the researcher in a better direction. Blackfoot documents as such will not be found, in the east, so acquiring as much local history as part of one's knowledge base will keep one's research on track.

DeMarce points out that the following nations of Indians contributed to the tri-racial isolate groups:

Chickahominy, Gingaskin, Mattaponi, Nansemond, Nanticoke, Nottaway, Pamunkey, Rapahanocks, Saponi, Weanick, Werowocomo.

There are some specific surname patterns that appear in the tri-racial communities. DeMarce cautions the researcher to avoid concluding too hastily that a relationship exists, just because the surname is the same. Yet on the other hand, she acknowledges that a specific pattern of name dispersal in a limited population may truly indicated which groups might be considered as isolates. As a result, her illustration of the tendency of the groups to intermingle among other similarly mixed groups and not on a regular basis to re-marry into the original racial groups makes them not only isolated from their original racial groups but also identifies them as isolate groups.

Chapter 11

Additional Records

For Black Indian Research

Chapter 11

Additional Records for Black Indian Research

To enhance the genealogical research of the African-Native American family, it is essential to become acquainted with as many documents as possible that pertain to the Five Nations, as well as those documents that might reflect Indian ancestry in other areas as well.

It has already been noted that the largest set of records pertaining to "Black Indians" lies with those from the Five Civilized Tribes. The most familiar are those of the Dawes Commission. Most of these records can be found on microfilm at the National Archives, or can be borrowed through many of the lending libraries around the country.[1]

However, additional documents exist and some of these can be obtained only at the National Archives in Washington, or Ft. Worth, while others are available only at center such as the Oklahoma Historical Society Archives in Oklahoma City, and in local courthouses in Oklahoma. Some of these records have never been microfilmed; therefore the researcher must be prepared to travel in order to obtain copies of these documents.

For example, individuals with Cherokee Freedmen ancestry are particularly fortunate because a unique set of valuable records exist for them. These are the Affidavits from the information pertaining to the Wallace Rolls were taken. The Wallace Rolls pertain primarily to the Cherokee Freedmen, and they contain the names of many who were

---

[1] The original records from the Dawes Commission are at the Federal Records Center in Ft. Worth Texas.

admitted on the Final Rolls. Other census records exist such as the Kern Clifton, the Dunn Roll and the Drennen rolls, but they vary in what they contain on the Freedmen, if anything at all. All of these earlier rolls hold value however, because in some cases the Freedman family has blood ties to the Indian family, or in other cases, the researcher still will want to follow the slave owner's family and often the Indian slave owner will be found on some of the other earlier rolls.

Special Freedmen Records

Because of an interesting arrangement that the Cherokees had with their freedmen and indeed with all who were seeking enrollment, there were several census counts taken from the time just after the Civil War, until the Final Dawes Rolls were prepared. Most of these other census rolls were not considered *official* by the end of the Dawes Commission enrollment process but they were used to see if the applicant had truly been in the territory, and were not intruders. The information found in the Affidavits from the Wallace Rolls should be studied, because they are a valuable source of additional information. In some cases, the files are completed on preprinted forms, while in other cases, the files are rather lengthy and can have some valuable data. In the case of Mary Johnson (see illustration), it is learned that she was originally born in Virginia, but then "stolen" and taken into the Cherokee Nation. The document was created in 1889 and she was 90 years old at that time. By her age, it is most probable that she traveled westward, as a slave, on the "Trail of Tears" during removal.

Unfortunately these affidavits are not on microfilm. The original affidavits are available only at the National Archives in Washington D.C., which limits the opportunities for those who live far away from that facility. However, it is

important for those researching Cherokee Freedmen
ancestors to become familiar with them. Even if one has

United IND. TER. }
CHEROKEE NATION

Before me. JOHN W. WALLACE, United States Commissioner, personally appeared
Mary Johnson who, after being duly sworn, states. My name
is *Mary Johnson* My age *90*. I was born in . . . . *Virginia*
. . . . I was a *Slave* at
the breaking out of the war of the Rebellion. My master's name was *Ben Johnson*
I was *in Cher. Nation*
. . . . . . at the breaking out of the war of the Rebellion.
I obtained my freedom by the Emancipation Proclamation. At the close of the war I was *in the*
State of Kansas . . . . I returned to the Cherokee Nation *1865* .
I now reside *Saline Dist C.N.* I am *not* a recognized voter. I am
married. My — is — a native and recognized citizen of the Cherokee Nation. I have
children. Their names and ages —

Given under my hand this 16" day of
Sept 1889

Mary X Johnson

Subscribed and sworn to before me
this 16th. day Sept. A.D. 1889

Jno. W. Wallace.
U.S. Commissioner.

Affidavit of Mary Johnson from the Wallace Roll Affidavits

located ancestors on the Dawes Rolls, they were probably on the Wallace Rolls and the affidavits might give more information. In many cases the affidavits reflect movement patterns of the freedman family especially during the Civil War and the period immediately following the War.

Here is a list of other records to use in one's search listed by tribe:

Cherokee Nation
1867 Tomkins Foll of Cherokee Freedmen
1880 Wallace Roll of Cherokee Freedmen including the Orphan Roll
1880 Cherokee Colored Persons whose names appear on the Clifton Roll but are not on the authenticated Roll of 1880
1890-1893 The Wallace Roll of Cherokee Freedmen
1896 Cherokee Freedmen Census (Including the following districts: Canadian, Cooweescoowee, Delaware, Flint, Going Snake, Illinois, Saline, Sequoya, and Tahlequah. The census contains records of adopted whites, Delaware Shawnees, and Freedmen)

Chickasaw Nation
Choctaw Chickasaw Freedmen 1896

Choctaw Nation
1885 Choctaw Chickasaw Freedmen Rolls
1896 Choctaw-Chickasaw Census

Creek Nation
1867 Citizens and Freedmen of the Creek Nation (Dunn Roll)
1867 Creek Freedmen Roll
1869 Pay Roll of Creek Freedman as of 1867

Seminole Nation
1901-1902 Allotment Schedules for Seminoles

Federal Census Records
     The use of Federal Census records should never be discounted when conducting Black Indian research. It is often assumed that one should look for tribal rolls as soon as the search for an Indian ancestor begins. Actually there is much benefit that one can gain from researching the Federal census.
     In 1900, Indian Territory was included in the official Federal Census of the United States. The two census years 1900 and 1910 provide some interesting information for the researcher, and can open new doors for the freedmen researcher. In 1900 and in 1910 there was a special inquiry, which was directed to Indians that did not pertain to the remainder of the U.S. population. For example, information is provided about the number of wives of the head of household in addition to information about the degree of Indian blood possessed by each household member. The case of the Freedmen can be quite interesting, because it is possible to find a freedman family listed in the 1900 census as black and in the 1910 census as Indian.[7]

     In the case of Samuel Walton from the Choctaw Nation, in 1900 the family appears as a black family living in the Choctaw Nation. Samuel, his wife Sallie, their sons Samuel and Houston are in the household as well as Sallie's brother Joe. In 1910, Houston, the son had passed away, and brother Joe had moved away leaving Samuel his wife Sallie and Son Sam. Their name appears this time on a special Indian census schedule along with a breakdown of the

---

[7] See Walton documents in Appendix 1, page 181-182

percentage of Indian blood of the family. In addition, other questions are also asked of the family.

For many black researchers, this information will hold special significance because the issue of blood is addressed. During the enrollment process for the freedmen of the Five Civilized tribes, the amount of Indian blood was never raised, thereby eliminating the freedmen from consideration as Indians by blood. This designation as "freedmen" and not as citizens "by blood" also gave the freedmen smaller allotments and payments by their respective nations.

For those whose ancestors appear on any of the Special Indian census pages there is an opportunity to learn about the racial mixture that may have existed in the family. It is emphasized that the degree of Indian blood is not the most critical information for the researcher, but it is mentioned because it is an interesting piece of data that appears after the nations had deliberately sought to eliminate this information during the enrollment process.

Data from the Indian 1910 Census Schedule

Information highlighted in the Indian census schedule consists of the following:

- Tribe of this Indian
- Tribe Mother
- Tribe of Father
- Degree of Indian Blood, (whether Indian, White, Negro)
- Is this Indian Living in Polygamy (Yes or No)
- Type of Dwelling of Family (Teepee or "Civilized")
- Is this Indian Taxed (Yes or No)

A Word about Slave Schedules

Because many Indians in Oklahoma were slave owners, the slave schedules from Indian Territory are useful. Much can be learned about what kind of enslavement that the enslaved ancestor may have experienced. Like the old south, there were slave owners in the various tribes with very large estates, and sizeable plantations, and at the same time, there were small slave owners who had only a few servants who lived with them. Since the slave owner was identified on the Dawes Rolls, then going to the slave schedule will be provide a good insight into how many other persons may have lived as slaves alongside one's ancestor.

Oklahoma Records

The value of traveling to Oklahoma to enhance one's research cannot be over-emphasized. A plethora of records exist for the freedmen researcher who dares to explore the resources in that states. At the Oklahoma Historical Society Archives in Oklahoma one will find a plethora of documents to explore one's history. Among the thousands of documents that are included, one will find Dawes records, marriage records, tribal court records, and early Oklahoma newspapers, to mention only a few of the resources. The courthouses in each county will hold marriage records, divorce records, and guardianship records, and many resources for researching land records.

The researcher is urged to become very familiar with the geography of Indian Territory as well as current Oklahoma. Known where the family lived before and after statehood, will provide some interesting information regarding land allotments. For example, the courthouse in

LeFlore County, Oklahoma held a land patent for Samuel Walton, Choctaw Freedmen and the receipt of 40 acres of land in what is now Poteau Oklahoma. Samuel Walton received these 40 acres, and information about his status as a Choctaw Freedman appears at the top of the patent. Many other courthouses hold similar documents in the land records. To find such documents, one must be able to identify the former residence of the ancestors in Indian Territory, and find the same community in the appropriate county in current day Oklahoma. There are many maps available of Indian Territory, and it is worthwhile to have both old territorial maps and a good current one of Oklahoma.

One is strongly encouraged to become familiar with the journal published by the Oklahoma Historical Society, *The Chronicles of Oklahoma*. In this quarterly journal are countless articles pertaining to Oklahoma's history, including some enlightening articles about the Freedmen from the five tribes.

Rejected Files

All who applied for enrollment were not admitted. Thus, several hundred records await black genealogists, whose ancestors were not admitted to any nation, who nevertheless went through a thorough interview process. There are records that parallel the previously mentioned ones (Enrollment cards, Applications for enrollment), but because the family was eventually not admitted for enrollment, there were stored under a different category.

The information in these files, in some cases, reveal far more detail than are those who were admitted to the nations. It also isn't unusual to find one set of family members who were admitted to a specific tribe while a sibling or a child was denied citizenship. These records are no less valuable than the records of those who were admitted to the Five Tribes.

Military Records in Black Indian Research

It is essential to take particular note of the value of military records, particularly for those whose ancestors may have come from the Cherokee and Creek nations. A large number of Black and Indians fled from the Cherokee and Creek nations into Kansas, early in the Civil War. Some of the blacks were free people, who fled into Kansas to avoid the conflict. Others left as slaves as conflicts were more intense, and others traveled as slaves with a large contingent of followers of Creek leader Opothole Yahola. This is often referred to as the Great Escape, a painful sojourn made in the icy winter of 1864, where many lives were lost. Hundreds of men, black and red, joined the military that year. Some were inducted in the 1st 2nd and 3rd Indian Home Guards as special Union soldiers.

Many others joined the 1st and 2nd Kansas Colored Infantry. They also ended up engaged in battle in the Civil War, and fought in many battles for the North. The soldiers in the Kansas Colored later became re-designated as soldiers in the United States Colored Troops as part of the 79th and 83rd U.S. Colored Infantry when they joined other slaves who had escaped to join those regiments from northwest Arkansas. After the Civil War ended, many of these soldiers returned to their homes in the Creek and Cherokee Nations.

As a result of their participation in the military, the survivors of those regiments applied for and received military pensions. The pension files are documents that hold a wealth of data for the genealogist, and Indian Territory researchers are encouraged to make sure that they survey the indexes of black Union soldiers for information of their participation. The online database known as the Soldiers and Sailors system is a useful and quick database to search for an ancestors's Civil War involement. It can be found at http://www.itd.nps.gov/cwss/soldiers.htm [3]

American Revolution

It is important to point out one of the few places that records might be found for persons whose ancestors lived free in the colonial era. There are records that pertain to the soldiers who served in the American Revolution. The Daughters of the American Revolution has published a very useful guide to researching and documenting African and Native American Ancestors who fought in the war of Independence. The publication is a useful one that belongs in the library of all Black Indian researchers, with ancestors from this era. The book is called: "Forgotten Patriots. African American and American Indian Patriots of the Revolutionary War. A Guide to Service, Sources, and Studies".

This work is recommended, because there is no other source of detailed information documenting the history of the participation of African Americans and American Indians in the Revolutionary War. The work also contains a valuable bibliography referencing thousands of citations. These citations will become very useful for the scholar researching this subject in more detail.

---

[3] *By using the database with a name such as Grayson, common in the Creek Nation, one will find over 20 names from Black Indian soldiers who served in either the Indian Home Guards or the United States Colored Troops.*

Documenting Indians in the 20th Century

Most researchers are familiar with the Federal Census Schedules. However, many are not aware that it is quite possible to document Indian families in those communities where they lived. In 1900 and 1910 the Federal Census acknowledged the large presence of Indian communities and actually placed census data on a special census schedule. In 1900 there was acknowledgement that there had been families that were mixed with white families. By 1910, the Federal authorities also provided census schedules that took into account the presence of communities of Indians that had contact with black families. As a result two special Indian census schedules were created, actually requiring the enumerator to record, if known, the percentage of Indian blood, white blood and black blood. The document cannot be considered to be a scientifically accurate document, however, it is an acknowledgment that there were communities of people who clearly had mixed with other races.

Therefore the Special Indian Census schedules should be used when conducting research. These census records are microfilmed as part of the regular census, but often found at the end of the "standard" census schedule.

On the top of the census schedule, the data on the special Indian census form resembles the traditional census schedule. Data is collected on persons in each household, reflecting name, age, relationship to the head of house, occupation, and place of birth. The bottom half of the Indian schedule records data pertaining to tribe, of person, their parents, and whether the person is considered to a "full blood" Indian, or mixed with another race.

155

1910 Special Indian Census
Left Side Portion of Indian Census Schedule[4]

Tribe of this Indian	Tribe of Father of this Indian	Tribe of Mother of this Indian	Proportion of Indian and Other Blood			Number of Times Married	Whether now living in polygamy	If living in polygamy, whether the wives are sisters.
			Indian	White	Negro			
33	34	35	36	37	38	39	40	41

This is a partial glimpse at the bottom half of the Special Indian Census, that records information on the racial composition of the family being enumerated. Note the special inquiries pertaining to the marital status.

---

[4] This is a blank census form provided by the National Archives
http://www.archives.gov/genealogy/census/native-americans/1910-data-collection-sheet-1.pdf

1900 Special Indian Census[5]

TWELFTH CENSUS OF THE UNITED STATES: 1900
SPECIAL INQUIRIES RELATING TO INDIANS

NATIVITY		MIXED BLOOD	CONJUGAL CONDITION	Cl
Tribe of Father of this Indian	Tribe of Mother of this Indian	Has this Indian any white blood; if so, how much? (0, ½, ¾, etc.)	Is this Indian, if married, living in polygamy?	Is this Indian taxed?
31	32	33	34	35

This illustration of the 1900 census reflected only family mixtures of Indian and white

[5] Ibid

Additional Data on 1900 Form:

BLOOD	CONJUGAL CONDITION	CITIZENSHIP			DWELLINGS
Indian blood; if much? ₄ etc.)	Is this Indian, if married, living in polygamy?	Is this Indian taxed?	Year of acquiring citizenship	Was citizenship acquired by allotment?	Is this Indian living in a fixed or in a movable dwelling?
3	34	35	36	37	38

This census schedule also records information on the dwelling of the person being enumerated.

Interpreting the Indian Census Schedules

It must be emphasized that the racial percentages recorded do not represent any kind of scientific or authentic representation for Indian blood. In some cases the enumerators simply guessed by looking at people. In other cases they made a mathematical calculation based on information provided to them.

The instructions to the enumerators deserve studying to comprehend that the racial designations was at best, an estimate made by the census taker. Note the illustration that follows:

COLUMN 33. – If the Indian has no white blood, write 0. If he or she has white blood, write ½, ¼, etc. whichever fraction is nearest the truth.

COLUMN 34. – If the Indian man is living with more than one wife, or if the Indian woman is a plural wife or has more than one husband, write "Yes." If not, write "No." the Indian is single, leave the column blank.

CITIZENSHIP. – If the Indian was born in this country, no entry can be made in columns 16, 17, or 18; but for columns 35, 36, and 37 answers must be obtained. If the Indian was born in another country, answers will be made both in columns 16, 17, and 1 and in columns 35, 36, and 37, in accordance with the facts.

COLUMN 35. – An Indian is considered to be "taxed" if he or she is detached from his or her tribe and living among white people as an individual, and as such subject to taxation, whether he or she actually pays taxes or not; also if he or she is living with his her tribe but has received an allotment of land, and thereby has acquired citizenship; in either of these two cases the answer to this inquiry is "Yes."

An Indian on a reservation, without an allotment, or roaming over unsettled territory, is considered "not taxed," and for such Indians the answer to this inquiry is "No."

The instructions regarding column 33 state "If the Indian has no white blood, write 0. If he or she has white blood write ½, ¼, etc. whichever fraction is nearest the truth.[6]

In the 1910 Indian census the instructions are even more complicated:

---

6   Ibid

The instructions for 1910 clearly stated:

> **Columns 36, 37, 38. Proportions of Indian and other blood.—**
> **If the Indian is a full-blood, write "full" in column 36 and leave columns 37 and 38 blank. If the Indian is of mixed blood, write in columns 36, 37, 38 the fractions which show the proportions of Indian and other blood as "column 35, Indian ¾ (column, white) ¼ and (column 38, Negro) 0 For Indians of mixed blood all three columns should be filled, and the sum in each cases should equal 1 as ½, 0, ½; ¼, 0, ¾; 1/8, 1/8; etc.**
>
> **Whenever possible, the statement that an Indian is of full blood should be verified by inquiry of the older men of the tribe, as an Indian is sometimes of mixed blood without knowing it.**

Again, it must be emphasized that the data recorded should not be considered to be scientifically accurate, because it many cases the enumerator was merely guessing. However, these two special Indian census schedules are included because they were used in multiple states, including New York, New Jersey, Pennsylvania, Virginia, North Carolina, South Carolina, Florida, Mississippi, and Oklahoma.

Additional Census years reflecting Indians
In later census years, Indian communities were also documented. There are different ways in which Indians were enumerated in the census.

1850 Census[7]
This is the first census to list all family members and record information about each person. People are identified as white, black, or mulatto; although in rare instances as Indian. There was no census in Indian Country (most of the mid-West)

1860 Census
There was not a large effort to identify Indian people in this census year. Racial designations were usually white, black or mulatto. There were occasionally some reflections of *Ind,* or *I* in the census.

1870 Census
Those known to be Indian were identified officially as Ind or I. There were some reservations that were identified during this census year.

1880 Census
This followed the same pattern as 1870.

1900 Census
Those who lived on "reservations" were identified for the first time in the federal census schedules. The special Indian census was used for the first time. (see illustrations)

1910 Census
Indians were recorded in the Special Indian census as well as showing up on the general population schedules.

1920 Census
When it was known, many were identified as *Indian* or *Ind* on the regular census schedules. There was no longer any special Indian census.

---

[7] Ibid

1930 Census
If one was enumerated as Indian it was noted in the 12th
column. There was also a "degree" of Indian blood
recorded.

School Records
Some records of Indian Schools are available to the public,
but not in large numbers. Many of the microfilmed Indian
school records pertain to the business or running the schools
with sparse information about the students themselves.

However, it is worthwhile to note that some of the Indian
schools were enumerated on the special Indian census
schedules, such as the Carlisle Indian School. The tribal
background of the pupils are recorded.[8]

---

[8] More than 50 pages exist for the Carlisle Indian School. Among the
pupils enumerated were some who were mixed Indian and black who
were from Massachusetts.

Chapter 12

Avoiding Pitfalls in Black Indian Research

Chapter 12

Avoiding the Pitfalls in Black Indian Research

There are many things that heave been mentioned in this text suggesting documents and resources to conduct one's genealogical research whether from the Five Civilized Tribes or from elsewhere. Occasionally one does hit the brick wall, and become blocked with no clear direction on where to go next. Here are four final rules to follow that might assist the Black Indian Researcher in documenting the family history.

Follow the Trail of Names, and Avoid the Search for Gold.

Many times one hears that a friend or colleague has begun to research their family history because they want their son or daughter to get an Indian scholarship. Or there is the case of the genealogist hoping to prove Native American ancestry for what is perceived to be Indian money coming one's way, if one can just prove that they have an Indian ancestor. This researcher who is following the "gold rush" for Indian money will follow a path that will quickly put their research on a road with a quick and permanent detour.

I recall while visiting the Oklahoma Historical Society Archives several years ago, I sat next to a gentleman, looking at the some Dawes records. He was researching Choctaw records intensely, and pouring through microfilm steadily. The assistant found some documents that he wanted of an ancestor and asked if he wanted to also have the testimony of his ancestor's sister. He did not, as he preferred to stay on the straight line of his gr. grandfather, that he was on. I was surprised that he did not want the gr. aunt's narrative for additional clues to the family history. I introduced myself and said that I was glad to meet another person researching Choctaw Freedmen. He leaned over to me, and whispered, "I am trying to get some of that Choctaw money!" He continued with his search, scrolling through hundreds of microfilmed images. There was no more need for dialogue, as he was busy with his frantic search for gold---Indian money. The assistant asked him a second time, if he wanted the info on the gr. grandfather's sister, and he said no. This time, he explained that he was on his gr. grandfather's trail, and wanted to stay focused. He was, but would never find what he was seeking because he was on the money trail. He had already fallen off of the genealogical trail when he joined the gold rush for perceived Indian money.

The man that I met frantically wanting to get his Indian money is not very different from some researchers who are looking for free scholarships or grants that they assume will come their way once they can prove that they are part Indian. This endeavor is not only fool-hardy, because one assumes that funds are coming forth to a person who has had no ties to any Indian community, or culture, and who has only a remote tie through an ancestor not remembered. There is an assumption that documenting one's history is an admission ticket into the tribe, to be followed by eligibility for a coveted scholarship.[1]

Such an endeavor is also one that is morally suspect. Being motivated by money, and not by a desire to document

---

[1] It should be pointed out that there are current political issues pertaining to admission to the Five Tribes. Freedmen descendants have become disenfranchised from the tribes, and several actions have arisen involving a number of lawsuits against the Seminole and Cherokee Nations. One's genealogy should not be lost in a quest for membership. At the same time, should one be seeking membership in one of the tribes, one will have to document one's genealogy to prove connection to the tribe, and a clear understanding of the Dawes records and its components will be essential.

history will take one off the genealogical trial very quickly and can literally bring one's research to an abrupt halt.

Keep the focus on the records, instead of physical features.

High cheekbones do not identify one of Indian ancestry. It is quite common to hear about the gr. grandmother with the high cheek bones, the proverbial long straight black hair, "so long she could sit on it", and other attributes that are sometimes Hollywood inspired images of what Indians look like. Long straight hair is characteristic of Europeans, Asians, and other people worldwide, and having an ancestor with such features is not genealogical proof of having Indian Ancestry.

There are some African Americans who will see the light skinned relative who was known to have had a white parent, with straight hair, hazel eyes, and will convincingly state that the ancestor was "part" Indian. This is no different from persons who are white, with a photo of an elder, or ancestor with identifiable Negroid features, and then label their *mulatto* ancestor as *Indian*.

Often the Indian family myth originates from persons who wish to disassociate themselves from a targeted racial group for whom there is little esteem. However, the research is what will take you to a better understanding of your history and heritage, not a labeling of a racial category based on skin tone, hair length or facial structure.

There are cases where persons, in the colonial era were identified for having a bi-racial background, who were white and Indian who were identified as *mulatto*. Some persons called *mulatto* were also black and Indian. However, there are other records created during that person's lifetime that may corroborate their background. When one researches, one must use a variety of records—tax records, court records, probate records, deeds, land records, old newspapers as well as the use of Federal records, and historical manuscripts for as much information in as many sources as possible. If the ancestor was indeed of native ancestry at least *one* of those records in which the ancestor's name appears will indicate this. When none of these records reflect Indian ancestry, there may be a reason.

Call your ancestors what they were. Avoid the "Blackfoot factor".

There are many names out there that one hears in reference to Indian ancestors, with the most common one being Blackfoot. There are the Cherokee Blackfoot, and the Blackfoot Cherokee, Cherokees of the South, Creeks of the Yamasee, and on and on.

If one's research is sound, one will quickly find the need to identify the accurate name by which ancestors were called. The desire to claim Native American ancestry is such a strong one, that a number of groups have been created, by eager and sometimes well meaning people, but historically however they are not real, and should have no part in the of documentation your ancestry. If your ancestors lived in the region of the Muskogee Creek people, then calling them Blackfoot will not put you on the right path in your research.

The *Blackfoot factor* in genealogy is a puzzling one, especially since there are new efforts to suggest that this designation refers to small tribes who lived in certain communities of the Saponi people.[2] If one is truly of native origin, there are some records someplace that refer to the people who eventually lived there, and there can be found references to persons in historical records of that region. There is no need to invent other groups that did not exist, or to call them by designations that they did not call themselves. You may be more likely to locate ancestors by the name they called themselves, rather than by an evolved designation that is historically inaccurate.

If the research is truly a sound genealogical search, the Blackfoot search comes to a dead end. In the lands east of the Mississippi, there are no Blackfoot rolls, no treaties with Blackfoot people, no Blackfoot villages. The Carolinas, Georgia, or other parts of the south do not reflect any settlements of Blackfoot Indians.

This search for the Blackfoot may be part of a colloquial expression, to describe one's family, however, sound research will tell who the family really was. Also when challenged, those who speak about the Blackfoot ties, will not really stick to the Blackfoot ancestor story. Very quickly in defense, the high cheek bone/long hair story will surface, and one will admit they don't know what tribe grandma was except that she was Indian.

It is quite possible that some of the now extinct Indian groups might indeed be an ancestral group from which one's family comes—so research that history, and follow the paper trail. The Blackfoot may not be found, but the family will.

---

[2] One of the many websites that discusses the probable origins of the southern tribes referred to as *Blackfoot* can be found at: http://www.saponitown.com/ . The site also provides other links to discussions about this subject.

Maintain the integrity of your research. Avoid Invention.

At a recent family reunion, an Arkansas family celebrated its history. A beautiful reunion booklet was produced telling the story of their Cherokee grandmother who was part of their family line. Their African ancestor, a runaway slave married a Cherokee woman, who taught him her customs and together, they raised a large family on the banks of the Arkansas River. The story is a beautiful one. It was also completely wrong.

Ironically the family above actually does have ties to the Cherokee Nation. The mother's side of the family was deeply a part of Chcrokee history and culture, and the some family land sits to this day on old Cherokee land allotments.

The mother of this Arkansas family had both parents who were original Dawes enrollees, on the rolls of the Cherokee Freedmen. A generation farther back, was a Civil War soldier who served in the United States Colored troops, who applied for and receive a notable pension for his role as a Union soldier. However, in an effort to embrace the Cherokee grandmother, the family walked past this rich history, to invent another story that never happened, and that historically was not possible, with the social and political obstacles in place in the 19th century.

How did the story get so mixed up? The father's side of the family was where the Cherokee grandmother myth started. The mix up was in place, for one reason, the father was the more "Indian looking" of the parents.

The mother of this family clan, was a dark skinned woman, was considered to be the "Negro"of the family, and the father, clearly of a mixed background was considered the

170

Indian. Yet, the reality is that the mother, who was of African ancestry, had an historical and genealogical tie to the Cherokee Nation, but an incorrect assumption left only one option when the reunion celebration arrived---they invented the story.

The real story of the family history makes the others story evaporate as it provides rich historical data, dozens of pages of documents from the Dawes records, to Civil War records.[3] Having chosen to invent the story of the runaway slave and the Indian maiden, took the family down a path that had a sudden end. There was, after all, no Cherokee maiden, no name, no place, and no proper historical concept. Simple basic research would prove that the gr. grandfather who was supposedly the runaway slave, was born a decade after the Civil War, and never could have been a runaway slave.

The effort to document family history is a rewarding venture, but not without its challenges. Documenting African American history is even more involved, for it involves identifying the enslaver, and then researching his or her lineage as well. Add to that, the challenges that one will encounter when beginning to research African and Native American families.

There are some records that will be useful for researchers from Oklahoma. However, those readers whose ancestors are from other tribes especially in the east will have their challenges. The extensive rolls are not as abundant for some tribes, and in other cases, evidence of indigenous people were obliterated intentionally. In some

---

[3] There is a very high rate of persons on the Dawes rolls, from the Cherokee and Creek Nations who served in the Indian Home Guards or the U.S. Colored Troops in the Civil War. The military records should be a critical part of the research process as well.

places native people were counted as mulatto or black, and in other places as white. In some cases their identities changed over the years. For example, in North Carolina, persons enumerated as Croatan, in 1900, are later referred to as Lumbees, and others from some of the nations in Virginia were simply terminated on paper and referred to as white, black or mulatto, with no references to their cultural identity

However, it is essential that as much thorough documentation as possible be used for the researcher, and a close adherence to the authentic names used by the communities to describe themselves are very important. And adherence to sound genealogical methodology will keep the researcher on track and will prevent derailing.

There is still much to be explored in Black Indian genealogical research. The efforts to document a tie to specific tribes can only be done when there are records that survive to use in this search. The Oklahoma records are extensive as are some of the Eastern records as well.

This work is a reflection of the lessons learned in the first years after the initial publication of *Black Indian Genealogy Research*, in 1993. There are other records to pursue, and other avenues to explore. The community of genealogists who explore Indian records is a small one, and the few that specialize in exploring African-Native families is a smaller one.

However, by adhering to sound methodology, keeping the integrity of the research in focus, the journey will be a successful one that will take the researcher down new paths.

Appendix 1

Documents
From Federal Census
Reflecting Black Indians

1900 Federal Census, Choctaw Nation

In 1900, the Walton Family was enumerated as black family residing in the Choctaw Nation. They had already gone through the Dawes enrollment process and had were awaiting approval for enrollment and later land allotments.

1910 Federal Census

In 1910, the Choctaw Freedman Walton family was enumerated on the Special Indian census schedule. The Waltons were enumerated in the regular population census in 1900, as a black family, as seen on the previous page. Note that in 1910, the bottom half of the page shows a percentage of Indian blood of the family members.

A close up of the record is on the following page. The Special Indian census schedule was used not only in Oklahoma, but also in select parishes of Louisiana, some counties in Mississippi, as well in places like North Carolina, where there was a sizeable Indian population. These Indian census pages are often found at the very end of the enumeration of the general population, therefore, when one cannot locate a family in the community, it is advised that these special records be examined.

1910 Close Up of Special Indian Census

In this closer view of the Special Indian Census, the Walton family is listed on the first three lines. They are now listed as an Indian family, and no longer as black. The bottom half of the document actually reflected a percentage of Indian blood of the persons in the household. (Sallie's brother is no longer residing in the household by 1910.)

Close View of Bottom Half
of 1910 Indian Census Schedule

The bottom half of the 1910 Indian Census Schedule reflects the percentage of Indian blood. The Walton family was reflected on the first three lines of the top half and their Indian blood is reflected on the first 3 lines of the bottom portion of the same document. Note that Samuel is said to have been ½ Cherokee, and ½ Negro. Sallie's blood is reported to be ¼ Choctaw and ½ Negro. In other states, similar documents also reflect mixtures of white, Indian or Negro.

178

Appendix 2

Surnames from the 1900 Federal Census Enumerated as Indian

For the South and Upper South

Arkansas, Alabama, Florida, Georgia Louisiana, Kentucky, Mississippi, North Carolina, South Carolina, Tennessee, Virginia

Surnames from 1900 Federal Census Enumerated as Indian

Because of a strong interest in persons knowing about Indian families of the south and upper south, this list represents a compilation of names made from indexes from the 1900 Federal census. The year 1900 was selected, because it was taken at the turn at the beginning of the 20th centuries. There were still households where persons were clearly identified, as being of native ancestry, and many of the deliberate efforts to eliminate the Indian designation that would unfold in a few short years, had not yet occurred. The names are therefore presented here, as a mere guide. Further research with sound genealogical methodology would be required to verify one's historical tie to any specific Indian nation.

Note: In some states, some Indians were enumerated only with a given name and without surname. In those cases, the single names are listed before the surnames for those states.

Alabama:	Hathcock	**Arkansas**
Adams	Jackson	Alexander
Alexander	Manac	Bates
Arington	Mccants	Bell
Bruce	McGhee	Breedlove
Cartarpen	Peacock	Brooks
Chambers	Preslcy	Clark
Colbert	Roland	Cockran
Crocket	Rolin	Crofford
David	Simpson	Fish
Dees	Steadham	Hatfield
Eleza	Walker	Heflin
Fisher	Wydees	Hunter
Hallinger	Woods	Johnson

181

Leon
Littledeer
Lyon
Morgan
Nofire
Porter
Pritchet
Ridge
Sampson
Shade
Sieckey
Standingdeer
Stanton
Standingdur
Stewart
Van Janton
Willie

Florida
(63 people
listed with no
name)
(Single names)
Annie
Canaca
Chicica
Chipce
Courtney
Emmer
Enalocktee
Etlochee
Fanny
Farrow
Hermkin
Lepojkee
Lizzie
Lucy
Mahatlachie

Mary
Natachee
Nicopee
Noothannie
Old Charlie
Old Money
Old Putty
Old Tallahassee
Old Tommy
Pasedko
Snooks
Tellechchee
Tolaca
Wassisatkee
(Surnames)
Armstrong
Bigelow
Billy
Bowleg
Bowers
Boy
Brooker
Buster
Canosa
Catcher
Cather
Charlie
Custa
Cypress
Dixie
Doctor
Fewell
Free
Fripp
Hamey
Ingraham
Jacobbs
Jem

Jemmie
Johnnie
Jones
Jumper
Lee
Lanier
Lustab
Martin
Mckinley
Micco
Motlow
Osceola
Parker
Roberts
Smith
Stewart
Stranahan
Tallabasse
Tiger
Tigertail
Tommy
Truitt
Tucker
Turkey
Tustenugee
Waters
Weekepee
Willie
Wilson

Georgia
Bonds
Callens
Carder
Carter
David
Demsey

Hammond	Battise	Jupitser
Lowry	Berry	Lagattuta
Nelson	Bevie	Langley
Orendine	Blueeye	Lede
Oxendine	Blumbh	Lee
Waggoner	Brandis	Lewis
Woodle	Brandy	Lipp
	Buard	Lobson
Kentucky	Caselle	McDonald
Allen	Celestine	McMaher
Campi	Chaney	Moore
Cole	Charles	Mora
Fletcher	Cheney	Murphey
Hung	Colas	Navarro
Mccarty	Collins	Obe
Nickels	Conaway	Pale
Smith	Dapeomant	Paul
	Dardare	Pecot
Louisiana	Darden	Pierro
(Single names)	Dardin	Pitre
Emma	Darin	Polite
Emily	Davis	Polk
Isaac	Dominique	Poncho
Sally	Elam	Robertson
(Surnames)	Emily	Rodriguez
Abbott	Fonteno	Sampson
Alabama	Gautreaux	Sanders
Alabams	Gibson	Saul
Allen	Griffin	Sauls
Antoine	Harrison	Shoemakcr
Anton	Hebeesaba	Silwanna
Armelin	Hellestin	Simpie
Austin	Hensley	Stauff
Babin	Hinson	Tell
Baptist	Jackson	Tensas
Baptiste	Jeanpierre	Thompson
Batice	John	Tishe
Batties	Johnson	Tombero

Tovey
Vena
Verdin
Verdun
Vulcano
Wash
Wass
Wilkinson
Williams
Willis
Wilson

Mississippi
Adams
Alderman
Alex
Allen
Alx
Amis
Amos
Anderson
Arbi
Arkanson
Arnis
Baley
Barney
Bartis
Beako
Beaks
Bell
Bellis
Berks
Besson
Bill
Billey
Billie
Billy
Bingle

Bishop
Bob
Bonse
Booth
Boston
Boyd
Bren
Brokesholder
Brooks
Brown
Bull
Cambie
Campbell
Cates
Charley
Charlie
Chatham
Chitto
Choctaw
Chubbie
Chubby
Clements
Coleman
Cook
Cooper
Crosby
Dam
Daniel
David
Davis
Dennis
Denson
Dias
Dickerson
Dickerson
Dickson
Dixey
Dixon

Dock
Duris
Eckols
Edwards
Eime
Ellis
Evans
Fannie
Farmer
Favre
Febus
Fingly
Fobbus
Foley
Formbby
Fortun
Frank
Frazier
Frenchman
Frierson
Fubb
Gibson
Gill
Gilmore
Gipson
Golden
Guss
Hainlubb
Haiter
Hall
Harper
Harris
Hatistie
Hattenstie
Hawkins
Henry
Hickman
Hicks

Hopkins	Levis	Philip
Horcher	Lewis	Phillip
Hubby	Longley	Phillips
Hudson	Louis	Pichetubber
Hutson	Mack	Pishtubby
Igaas	Malay	Polk
Ind	Maly	Polly
Indian	Marris	Porter
Ingals	Martha	Post Oak
Isaac	Martin	Poxon
Isham	Martine	Price
Isom	Matliann	Quilian
Ivory	McCormick	Reed
Jack	McDonald	Reese
Jackson	McMilon	Rennie
Jackway	McArthur	Richmon
Jacob	McGee	Robinson
Jakway	McMellon	Robison
James	McWilson	Rodes
Janchron	Merris	Russell
Janes	Mike	Saeman
Jasper	Mitchell	Sam
Jeff	Monis	Sam
Jefferson	Morris	Sann
Jenn	Moss	Scott
Jim	Nancy	Seals
Jimpson	Neal	Sharmakes
Joe	Nicaly	Sheperd
John	Nubby	Shoemake
Johnson	Nubley	Shoemaker
Joshua	Oscar	Shutubby
King	Pack	Simpson
Labine	Packson	Smith
Ladner	Parker	Sociby
Lafontain	Past Oak	Socka
Lamgly	Peek	Sockey
Larmdeon	Peter	Solomon
Lee	Petis	Solomon

Spade
Stephens
Steve
Stoloby
Stout
Stribling
Sudiaur
Swiney
Tackls
Taylor
Thomas
Thompson
Tom
Tubby
Tuby
Tuckalo
Tucklow
Tuckalo
Urllis
Vaughn
Vond
Wainright
Walkin
Wallace
Wallan
Wallis
Washington
Watkins
Watts
Wesheark
Wesley
White
Whiteman
Wickman
Wicksom
Wickson
Wiley
Wilkerson

Wilkerson
William
Williams
Williamson
Willie
Willin
Willis
Wilson
Yerby
Yim
York

North Carolina
(Single names)
A-che-ne
Aee-cuh-ne
Ah cah noh
Ah co tee gah
Ah lee stah ne
Ah m-ke
Ah mah chain
Alsie
Annie
Arneech
Che wah ne
Coo lah ge
David
Dickson
Eve
Ezkiel
Ge-yah-stoh
Gene-e
Irene
Isaiah
Jennie
Joe
John
Kannee

Lacey
Loyd
Marinda
Mary E
Mos-well-no-w
Moses
Nah-lee-ne
Nannie
Ned
Oo wah w
Oo-w-moh alec
Qua-w-ye
Sah-tah-ge
Sakie
Sarah
Saw nook still
So-ke-ali
Sow nook polk
Spade
Stacy
Sunche
Swa ge
Tarquit
Taw ya nee tah
Will-no-w
Willie
(Surnames)
Allen
Allsie
Amanall
Arch
Armichain
Arne
Arneach
Arnochain
Ax
Axe

186

Backing Water
Baker
Ballard
Bams
Barder
Barns
Barton
Bastley
Bawe
Bayon
Bear
Beck
Bees
Beg-jim
Bell
Berry
Big Owl
Big gim
Bigmart
Bigmeal
Bigmeat
Bigmest
Bigweat
Biles
Bird
Black
Blackfox
Blank
Blanks
Blee
Blythe
Bolvins
Booke
Bowen
Bowers
Bowins
Boyd
Boyd

Braboy
Braby
Bradley
Bragdon
Braley
Brayboy
Brayfoy
Brewer
Brigman
Bringsnake
Broglin
Brooks
Brown
Bryant
Bullard
Burgess
Burnett
Bushyhead
Buwington
Call
Caloualeskah
Catalso
Catolsa
Campbell
Canady
Candies
Carlie
Carner
Carson
Carter
Cat
Catolsti
Catt
Cees
Chain
Chaous
Charas
Charest

Charis
Charles
Charleston
Charon
Chasmar
Chaun
Chavis
Chavous
Cheech
Chickallio
Chilktasken
Chiltawski
Clark
Climbing-bear
Cloud
Coats
Cohoun
Coleman
Colhoun
Collins
Collonabeeckib
Collonsheskib
Colosti
Comal
Comer
Comeue
Conady
Conley
Connick
Cormally
Corn
Conrselle
Cornsilk
Cotolsti
Cowaie
Cox
Craig
Crosson

Crow
Cuamber
Cucumber
Cumbo
Cummings
Cummins
Cunning
Cunnings
Dais
Darter
Daves
Davis
Deklear
Dees
Deese
Demong
Demory
Dewattley
Diac
Dial
Dickey
Dickie
Dobson
Doby
Dockham
Docklear
Driver
Dunlap
Dure
Eady
Edwards
Evans
Fayneta
Feather
Featherhead
Feilds
Fesant
Folk

Freeman
French
Garell
Gary
Gatley
George
Godwin
Going
Goins
Gorrie
Graham
Gray
Graybeard
Green
Grham
Grohorn
Gutoga
Hagans
Haiden
Hammond
Hammonds
Hammons
Hammonse
Hammson
Hamson
Hanman
Harden
Hardin
Harkin
Harman
Harmann
Harmon
Harris
Heatherly
Henderson
Hendrie
Herner
Hill

Hodges
Hombuckle
Hornbuckle
Horntrickle
Howard
Hucker
Huggans
Hummons
Hunt
Jackiah
Jackson
Jacob
Jacobs
Jake
Janes
Jeavons
Jeavons
Jessan
Jocklear
John
Johnson
Jollan
Jone
Jones
Jordan
Juhnensky
Jumper
Junaluskee
Junulsky
Keg
Kegg
Keley
Ketiska
Lackland
Lacklear
Lacklie
Lacklier
Lacklin

Lambert	Lockliar	Mcgirs
Lams	Locklier	Mcgirt
Laphear	Locklin	Mclackland
Larch	Locust	Mclean
Larkin	Lomie	Mcmillan
Larklear	Long	Mcwilliams
Larsh	Lonoie	Mike
Lassey	Lonon	Mink
Laswell	Loonia	Minor
Laubert	Lorklien	Mitchel
Laurie	Lossie	Mitchell
Law	Louary	Mithcel
Lawery	Louise	Moore
Lawrendenda	Lourie	Morgan
Lawson	Loven	Morrison
Leber	Lowary	Muirblehead
Lechlian	Lowen	Mumbbhead
Lecklier	Lowerly	Mumblehead
Ledford	Lowie	Murphy
Lee	Lowine	Natdoringwell
Lehroon	Lowis	Ned
Lennon	Lowni	Newell
Lenon	Lownie	Newlin
Lertha	Lowrey	Nickey Jack
Lervis	Lowrie	Nosary
Little	Loyd	Nottytown
Littlejohn	Luckcar	Ohannon
Loavier	Magnar	Okwataga
Lockcar	Maney	Ollion
Lockhar	Manor	Ong
Lockhart	Many	Oo-la-i-way
Locklair	Martin	Oo-sa-wee
Locklar	Maul	Oocumma
Locklea	Mayers	Oosowi
Locklean	Mcarthur	Orendim
Locklear	Mccage	Orendine
Lockleir	Mccay	Orenstein
Lockler	Mcgirk	Oscar-wee

Otter
Owl
Oxendine
Panther
Patridge
Peary
Pheasant
Pigeon
Pockless
Pone
Pongman
Porter
Powell
Qualy
Queen
Ransom
Ranson
Ratley
Rattler
Ratty
Reach
Reed
Revels
Richarson
Rodgers
Rody
Rovels
Runnon
Russell
Sacklie
Salola
Salole
Sam
Sambriij
Samper
Sampson
Sander
Sanders

Sanderson
Sannooace
Sannooke
Sarah
Sardison
Sarnook
Sarnooke
Sarnookee
Saup
Scott
Scramer
Screamer
Screomer
Sea-nooke
Sealy
Seapeafryah
Seay
Sequaysh
Sequiah
Shakear
Shell
Shelle
Sherrill
Shich
Sketiey
Skittie
Smith
Smoke
Sneed
Sneemer
Solola
Soloneta
Sonnooke
Sott
Sounook
Spaulding
Spencer
Spraldine

Stamper
Standing
Standingwater
Staudingdur
Stewart
Strickland
Stricklin
Strickling
Stroops
Sullaway
Sunderman
Sunderson
Swaney
Sweet
Swimer
Swimmer
Swinie
Talala
Talola
Taluskeh
Tarquit
Tayle
Tayler
Taylor
Tayneeta
Tewala
Thomas
Thompson
Tooniah
Toyheska
Tramper
Tromper
Troy
Turkey
Ute
Wade
Waggie
Wahhahoo

Walkingstick
Wallace
Walters
Wanekah
Wanneta
Warray
Washington
Wata
Water
Watkins
Watson
Watty
Wayne-will
Webb
Welch
West
Whippoorwill
White
Wildcat
Wilkins
Will
William
Williamson
Willison
Willnota
Wilusta
Woddle
Wolf
Wolfe
Wood
Woddell
Woddin
Woriax
Wright
Wynne
Yellow
Yona
Yonce

Young
Young Deer
Youngaur
Youngbird
Youngdeer

**South
Carolina**:
Ayres
Bartley
Bell
Blue
Bradley
Brayboy
Brown
Candy
Canty
Castia
Chavis
Coats
Fields
George
Gordan
Gordon
Harris
Hunt
Just
Lochsair
Locklear
Lockley
Lucy
Niece
Roberts
Ryan
Smith
Stephen
Ton
Watt

Wylie

Tennessee:
Boling
Bouldin
Canfield
ClarkConkin
Dodsin
German
Gibson
Goans
Goins
Harris
Jackson
Mcfaddin
McKenney
Mitchell
Murphy
Ross
Techeskey

**Virginia
(Single Names)**
Fanny
Lucy C
Mary
(Surnames)
Adams
Allmond
Archequette
Badger
Bailey
Baldwin
Bass
Bear
Bear Heart
Beauchamp
Beverly

Black Hawk
Blake
Blevens
Boss
Bradby
Bright
Brown
Burton
Clark
Collins
Creeks
Crosby
Dennis
Docter
Donald
Dow
Doxtater
Elm
Evans
Firetail
George
Gillelle
Glick
Godfrey
Ground
Heath
Hendricks
Howard
Hunter
James
Johnson
Jones
Lakock
Lambert
Lancaster
Lankston
Lee
Leeds

Leftwich
Leven
Leybon
Lodge
Madison
Mason
Medecine
Metoxen
Miles
Mine
Mitchell
Morgan
Murray
Nelms
Newton
Noel
Osborne
Page
Patterson
Pearman
Pemberton
Peters
Petulinni
Plummer
Poodry
Powless
Printup
Quinney
Rich
Roberson
Rogers
Ross
Sampson
Sanders
Sanwooke
Satiyopa
Selverhells

Seneca
Setting
Silas
Skenandore
Soldbumen
Spain
Spittog
St. John
Stiles
Subiston
Summerson
Surrounded
Swain
Swaney
Swead
Taylor
Thomas
Ukipata
Walf
Walter
Waterman
Weaver
Webster
Whalock
White
Whiteley
Williams
Williamson
Wizi
Wright
Wynn

Appendix 3

Freedman Surnames from the Final Rolls of the Five Civilized Tribes

Appendix 3

Freedman Surnames from
The Final Rolls
of the Five Civilized Tribes

These surnames are placed here merely as a guide for persons just beginning the search. They are listed by tribe, especially for those who are not certain in which nation to begin their quest. This does not contain additional surnames from the New Born or Minor Freedmen Rolls. In a majority of cases the infants held the same surname as the parent whose name was on the original roll

When looking at the Final Rolls of the Freedmen of the different nations, the surnames frequently appear in more than one nation. However, there were some interesting charac-teristics to note. For example, many Freedmen from the Cherokee Nation had the surname Ross. This is not unusual considering that Chief John Ross and his family were major slave owners. Likewise many wealthy Vanns in the Cherokee Nation also had many slaves. Joseph Vann owned over 100 slaves. In the Choctaw nation one of the more frequent surnames to ap pear among the Freedmen was Colbert. Many of these were former slave of Jincy Colbert. At the same time, there were many Freedmen who bore Indian surnames, although they were often single individuals rather than entire families. A very common name appearing with Seminole Freedmen was Cudjoe. This is particularly interesting because the name Cudjoe, (or Kudjoe, or Quadjo) is clearly a West African name very common in Ghana. There have been no studies on this, but keeping mind the Seminole history and their relationship with Africans, one might infer that many of the blacks in the Seminole Nation had a strong cultural tie to Africa, that the name somehow survived slavery and immersion into the Seminole culture. There are dozens of Cudjoe families who are descendants of the Seminole Freedmen and are scattered throughout Oklahoma, ans the western states. The following family names are groups alphabetically, by nation. Researchers are encouraged to note that many surnames appear in more than one tribe. Therefore if one is uncertain about which of the Five Civilized Tribes to search, it recommended that one look at surnames in each nation before beginning their research.

CHEROKEE FREEDMAN SURNAMES

A	Barden	Blair
Adair	Barker	Blake
Adams	Barlow	Blunt
Alberty	Barnes	Blythe
Aldrich	Beam	Bolin
Allen	Bean	Boone
Alrid	Beck	Boudinot
Alwell	Beeson	Bowles
Anderson	Bell	Bowlin
Amrstrong	Benge	Boyd
Arnsby	Benton	Bradford
Austin	Berlone	Brady
	Berry	Brannon
B	Bird	Braves
Baker	Birdsong	Break-bill
Baldridge	Blackhawk	Brewer
Ballard	Blackwell	Brown

Bruce
Bruner
Bryant
Buckler
Buckner
Buddgington
Buford
Burgess
Burney
Bursby
Burton
Byrd

C
Caesar
Caldwell
Calvin
Campbell
Canard
Carbin
Carr
Carson
Carter
Cates
Chambers
Charles
Chase
Chatman
Childers
Choate
Chouteau
Chukelaste
Claggett
Clark

Clay
Clifton
Clinch
Coast
Coker
Colbert
Colmean
Collins
Coody
Cooper
Cordrey
Cornish
Cotton
Cox
Crapo
Cravens
Crawford
Crippen
Crittendon
Crockett
Crossland
Crossley
Cruthfield
Curls
Curtis

D
Dalton
Daniels
Dansby
Davis
Dawn
Day
Dean

Deaton
Deckman
Delwood
DeMumber
Dennis
Derrick
Dickson
Diges
Dixon
Dotson
Dowing
Drew
Duncan

E
Eagle
Eastman
Eaton
Ebb
Edwards
Elliott
Ellis
Escoe
Evans

F
Fields
Fleeks
Flowers
Flynn
Folsom
Ford
Foreman
Foster

Francis
Frazier
Freeman
French
Fry
Frye
Fulsomje
Funkhauser
Funter

G
Gaines
Garlington
Garnett
Garrett
Gaskins
Gentry
Gibson
Gilds
Givens
Glass
Goff
Goldsby
Graves
Gray
Grayso
Green
Griffin
Grimmett
Grobes
Groomer
Grooms
Grye
Gunter

H
Haddox
hailstock
Hale
Hall
Hamilton
Hanks
Hardman
Hardrick
Harlan
Harland
Harlin
Harper
Harris
Hayes
Henderson
Hickey
Hicks
Hight
Hill
Holt
Homes
Hopkins
Howell
Hudson
Huff
Hughes
Humphreys
Humphries
Humphry
Hunter
Huston

I
Ireland
Irons
Irven
Ivory

J
Jackson
James
Jamison
Jenkins
Jimison
Johnson
Jones

K
Kell
Kelly
Kemp
Kernel
Keys
Kilpatrick
King
Kircum
Kirk
Kirby

L
Laflace
Landrum
Lane
Lang

Langston
Lasley
Ledman
Lee
Leek
Lephew
Lett
Lewis
Lilpe
Linsey
Little
Logan
Lorens
Litt
Love,
Lovely
Llowe
Lowery
Luckey
Luther
Lynch
Lyons

M
Mabry
Macken
Mackey
Mackum
Madden
Malven
Manley
Markham
Marshall
Martin

Martom
Mathews
Mayberry
Mayes
Mayfield
Mayo
McClure
McConnel
McConnell
McCoy
McCrackin
McCullough
McCurtain
McDade
McDaniel
McDaniels
McElroy
McLain
McNair
McQueen
McWaters
Meadows
Meigs
Melton
Merrell
Middleton
Milam
Miller
Minnus
Minsy
Mitchell
Monday
Moored
Morgan

Morris
Muldrow
Mundis
Munson
Murrell
Musgrove

N
Nalls
Nash
Nave
Nelson
Nero
Nivens
Nolen

O
Owens

P
Pack
Paine
Parker
Parks
Parris
Patterson
Pee
Penn
Pennington
Perry
Perrryman
Petit
Pettit

Piner
Poorboy
Porlar
Porter
Posell
Powell
Price
Purtle

R
Ragsdale
Ratcliff
Ray
Reed
Reese
Reeves
Reid
Reynolds
Richardson
Rider
Roach
Roberson
Robertson
Robinson
Rodgers
Roe
Rogers
Rose
Ross
Roster
Rowe

S
Sales
Sanders
Sango
Scarborough
Schaefer
Schrimsher
Scott
Shankling
Shannon
Shepard
Sehppard
Silk
Simmons
Skates
Slater
Smit
Snow
Spight
Stanton
Starr
Stidman
Stidmon
Still
Sumner
Sumpter
Sutton
Swan
Swepston
Sypkes

T
Taylor
Terry
Theodore
Thomas
Thompson
Thornston
Townsend
Tucker
Tyner

V
Van Zant
Vann

W
Wade
Wagoner
Walker
Wallace
Ward
Warren
Washington
Watie
Watkins
Watson
Wear
Weaver
Webb
Webber

Welch
Welcome
West
White
Whitemrie
Whitmire
Wickliff
Wiggins
Williams
Willis

Wilson
Winters
Wofford
Wolfre
Woodall
Woodard
Woods
Workman
Wright

Y
Young
Youngblood

Chickasaw Freedman Surnames

A
Abram
Alberson
Albert
Alexander
Alfred
Allen
Alop
Anderson
Armstrong
Augustus
Austin

B
Bachelor
Bailey
Barlow
Barr
Beasley
Bend
Bennett
Bice
Birt
Bishop
Black
Blackwater
Block
Blue
Bly
Bower
Boyd
Brashears
Brewer

Breyson
Bright
Brooks
Brown
Bruner
Buckler
Bullocks
Burden
Burney
Butler

C
Caldwell
Campbell
Carney
Carolina
Carroll
Carson
Carter
Cass
Charles
Chawano-
    chubby
Cheadle
Chery
Chesnut
Chico
Chief
Childs
Chitlow
Choate
Choice
Christian

Clark
Clay
Cobry
Cochran
Cohee
Coker
Colb
Colbert
Cole
Colly
Combs
Conley
Conly
Cook
Cooper
Covan
Cox
Crathers
Cravatt
Cravens
Crittenden
Crockett
Croomes
Crooms
Culpepper
Cunish
Curry

D
Daly
Daniel
Daniels
Danna

Daugherty
Davidson
Davies
Davis
Denmark
Dindy
Dinwidddie
Dixon
Doleon
Doser
Douglas
Douglass
Dumkas
Duncan
Dunford
Dyer

E
Eastman
Edwards
Eights
Elliott
Evans
Even
Everhart

F
Factor
Falless
Farroww
Findley
Finlay
Finley
Fisher

Fitchgerl
Flacks
Flint
Ford
Foreman
Forrester
Fort
Franklin
Frazier
Fulsom

G
Gaines
Gamble
Garrett
Gas
Gasper
Gates
Gentry
Gibbs
Fibson
Giles
Gillespie
Givens
Glover
Goff
Golden
Goldsmith
Gooden
Gooding
Gorden
Graham
Grant

Grayson
Green
Greenwood
Greer
Grey
Griffin
Grimmett
Gunn

H
Hall
Hamilton
Hampton
Harlan
Harper
Harris
Harry
Hawkins
Heard
Henderson
Hendersy
Hennesy
Hervey
Hines
Hodges
Holder
Homedy
Hooks
Horn
Hornbeak
Houser
Houston
Humby
Humdy

Humphreys
Huntley

I
Ingram
Irvins

J
Jackson
Jacobs
Jameson
Johns
Johnson
Jonas
Jordon
Joseph

K
Keel
Keep
Kelly
Kemp
Kennedy
Kersy
Kiah
Kimbale
Kingsberry
Kinrick
Kirk

L
Lamey
Lawrence
Leader

Lee
Lewis
Ligon
Lin
Lincoln
Lofton
Loftus
Love
Lynch

M
Mahardy
Manning
Martin
Mason
Mays
McCain
McClendon
McClish
McCoy
McDermott
McDonal
McGee
McGilbray
McKenzie
McKinney
McMillan
Merriman
Mike
Miles
Miller
Mimmus
Mintfield
Mitchell

Mohuntubby
Molton
Monroe
Montgomery
Moody
Moore
Morrow
Moses
Murray
Murry
Myers

N
Nail
Nance
Neel
Nero
Newberry
Nims
Noel
Nolitubby
North
Nowell

O
Ogles
Oldhom
Oscar
Owens

P
Paris
Parks
Patrick

Patton
Paul
Payne
Pearsey
Pendleton
Peoples
Perry
Peters
Pettus
Petty
Phillips
Pickens
Piggett
Plummer
Poe
Pollen
Porter
Powell
Powers
Preuilt
Price
Prince

Q
Quinn

R
Randolph
Reed
Reese
Reynolds
Richardson
Ridge
Riverts

Roberts
Roby
Rodville
Rollen
Rose
Ross
Roy
Russell

S
Sampson
Samuels
Scannon
Scott
Sealy
Sears
Shatubby
Shaw
Shell
Shirley
Shoeape
Smallwood
Smith
Sparks
Speer
Speers
Spencer
Stanfield
Stephen
Stevenson
Stevison
Stewart
Stroud

Sumers
Summers
Sutton
Swindle

T
Taylor
Tecumseh
Thomas
Thompson
Tipkins
Tobler
Toles
Townsend
Townsley
Towser
Triplett
Tutter
Twyman
Tyner
Tyson

U
Underwood

V
Van
Vanley
Vaughn
Vincent
Vollen

W

Wade
Walker
Walton
Ward
Washington
Waters
Watson
Watts
Wesley
Whaley
Wheeler
Whitaker
White
Whitson
Wilder
Wiley
Wilkerson
Wilkes
Wilkins
Wilkinson
Williams
Williamson
Willis
Wilson
Windom
Wolf
Woods
Worley
Wright

Y

Yates
Yocubby
Young
Younger

Choctaw Freedman Surnames

A
Abbott
Abram
Adams
Adamson
Ainsworth
Alberson
Alexander
Allen
Anderson
Arnold
Askew
Austin

B
Bagley
Bailey
Banks
Barber
Barley
Barr
Barrett
Barrows
Bary
Bassett
Battie
Battiece
Battiest
Beams
Bearden
Beavers
Beckwith

Beeson
Belcher
Bell
Belvin
Benson
Bibbs
Bidden
Biggs
Binks
Bird
Birdsong
Blackwater
Blair
Bledsoe
Blocker
Blue
Blunt
Boatwright
Boldin
Bolding
Bonham
Bordon
Bowers
Boyd
Boyles
Brack
Bradley
Brady
Brasco
Brashears
Brewer
Briggs

Briley
Brown
Bruce
Brumley
Bruner
Bryant
Buckman
Buckner
Buffington
Bulger
Burks
Burris
Burton
Busby
Butler
Byrd

C
Caephus
Cahill
Cain
Campbell
Carney
Carr
Carroll
Carson
Carter
Caruthers
Cass
Chalk
Chambers
Chandler

Chapman
Charry
Chatman
Cheadles
Chester
Chilton
Chism
Choate
Christian
Clarik
Clay
Clayton
Cleveland
Cochran
Cohee
Cohes
Colbert
Cole
Coleman
Colly
Conard
Cook
Cotton
Cos
Craig
Cravens
Crawford
Cris
Crittendon
Crooms
Croons
Crutchfield
Cubit
Culver

Cunford

D
Dana
Dangerfield
Daniels
Daugherty
Davis
Demps
Demus
Dizer
Dockins
Dodd
Dodson
Donegay
Dougla
Douglass
Duckett
Dumas
Duncan
Durant

E
Eastman
Easton
Edd
Edwards
Eights
Ellis
Ellison
Elridge
Epps
Ervin
Eubanks

Evans
Everdige
Evrett
Ewings

F
Factory
Farris
Featherspoon
Featherson
Ferguson
Fields
Finley
Fisher
Flack
Fleeks
Flint
Floyd
Folsom
Foreman
Franklin
Frazier
Freeman
Freeney
Freeny
French
Fullbright
Fulsom

G
Gables
Gafney
Galvert
Galloway

Gant
Garnder
Garland
Gay
Gibson
Giddens
Givens
Glover
Gooding
Goodlow
Graham
Graves
Gray
Grayson
Green
Greenwood
Greer
Gross
Grundy
Guess
Guest

H
Haley
Halford
Hall
Hampton
Hardlan
Harkins
Harnage
Harris
Harrison
Harvey
Hatley

Hawkins
Haywood
Henderson
Henry
Hester
Hicks
Hill
Hilliard
Hills
Hines
Hodges
Hogan
Holford
Hollaway
Hollin
Holt
Homer
Hoppy
Horn
Hornback
Horton
Hotchkins
Hotchkiss
Howell
Hughes
Humdy
Humes
Humphrey
Hunter
Hutchins
Hutchison
Hyatt

I
Ingram
Irving

J
Jackson
Jacob
Jamerson
James
Jeater
Jeffers
Jefferson
Jeffries
Jeter
John
Johnson
Johnston
Jolly
Jonyes
Jordon
Joseph
Judy
Justice

K
Keel
Keith
Kemp
Kendrick
Kendricks
Kincade
King
Kingsbury
Kirk

L
Larkin
Last
Lathers
Lawrence
Lawson
Lee
Leflore
LeFlore
Leftridge
Lenox
Leppord
Lewis
Liggins
Lison
Littlejohn
Livingston
Logan
Looney
Love
Lovelance
Low
Lowery
Lownen
Lynch

M
Mabry
Mackey
Mahardy
Mann
Manning
Mansfield
Mat-ub-bee

Maturby
Maupin
Mawell
May
Mayes
Myes
Maytubby
McAfee
McCarty
McChristian
McClendon
McCloud
McCoy
McCurtain
McDaniel
McDonald
McGee
McGilbry
McGuire
McKee
McKinley
McKinney
McNeill
McQuilla
Meggs
Merritts
Miles
Miller
Mills
Milton
Minner
Mitchell
Moore
Moors

Morgan
Morton
MosesMosley
Moss
Munn
Murchison
Murphy
Murray
Musgrove

N
Nail
Nash
Neal
Neighbors
Neill
Nelson
Newberry
Newton
Nolan
Noland
Nolen
Norman
Norris
Nouvle
Nunley
nunnally
Nunnely

O
Oats
Oliver
Osborn

Oscar
Overton
Owens
Owles

P
Paris
Parish
Parker
Parkins
Partilla
Patterson
Patton
Payton
Pearson
Pendleton
Perry
Phelps
Phillips
Pickens
Pierce
Pitchlynn
Pitner
Poleon
Powell
Pratt
Price
Prince
Pryor
Pulcher
Purdy
Pursley

R
Radford
Railback
Read
Record
Rector
Reddick
Reed
Reeder
Reeves
Rentie
Reynolds
Rice
Richards
Richardson
Riddle
Ridge
Riffington
Riley
Riston
Roberts
Robinson
Rogy
Roebuck
Rogers
Rose
Ross
Russell

Ssakki
Sams
Samuels
Sandridge
Scott

Seely
Sell
Severe
Exton
Shaw
Shelby
Shelton
Shephard
Shield
Shields
Shirley
Shoals
Sholes
Short
Sifax
Simmons
Simpson
Sims
Sindham
Smallwood
Smith
Spencer
Spring
Stakohaka
Stanley
Star
Starly
Starr
Stephenson
Stevenson
Stewart
Striblin
Stribling
Stubblefield

Suton
Sutton

T
Taylor
Teel
Thomas
Thompson
Thurman
Timpson
Tinkshell
Tis
Titus
Triplett
Tucker
Turner
Tyler
Tyner
Tyson

V
Valliant
Vaughn
Vinson
Virginl
Voyd

W
Wade
Wagoner
Waldron
Walford
Walker
Walter

Walton
Walzer
Ward
Ware
Warner
Warren
Warrior
Washington
Waters
Watson
Webb
Welch
West
Whitaker
Whitby
White
Wilburn
Wilkins
Williams
Willis
Wilson
Winbley
Wine
Woods
Wooten
Worthen
Wright

Y
Yocubby
Young

Creek Freedman Surnames

A
Abrams
Adams
Add
Adkins
Alberty
Alec
Aleck
Alex
Alexander
Allen
Andrew
Andy
Ard
Asbury
Atkins
Austin

B
Bailey
Baker
Ballard
Banks
Barer
Barker
Barnes
Barnett
Bernette
Bates
Batt
Batts
Bean

Beaver
Bell
Berry
Berryhill
Billy
Birney
Bishop
Blackburn
Blackstone
Boone
Bowleg
Bowlegs
Bowman
Boyd
Bradberry
Bradford
Brady
Brewster
Brinkley
Bristor
Broadnax
Brooks
Brown
Bruner
Buckner
Buffington
Bumpus
BunnBurgess
Burnett
Burney
BurtonButler
Byrd

C
Canada
Canard
Cannon
Carlina
Carnard
Carr
Carson
Carter
Ceasear
Chambers
Charles
Childres
Childs
Choteau
Clark
Clayton
Clinton
Coats
Cobb
Cobbrey
Cohee
Colbert
Cole
Coleman
Collin
Colling
Colly
Conner
Cooks
Coon
Corbray

Cousins
Cowans
Cox
Crabtree
Craig
Crane
Craw
Crossley
Crosslin
Cruel
Cudjo
Cudjoe
Cuff
Culley
Cully
Curns
Curtis
Cyrus

D
Dan
Daniels
Davis
Davison
Dean
Deleny
Deloney
Dennis
Derisaw
Dindy
Dixon
Doil
Dolman
Douglass

Downs
Doyle
Drake
Draper
Drew
Duff
Dunbar
Durant
Dyle

E
Easley
Easup
Eastman
Edwards
Epperson
Escoe
Eubanks
Evans
Everett

F
Factor
Faro
Faster
Fee
Fester
Fields
Fife
Fink
Fisher
Flannagan
Flint
Flowers

Flynn
Folsom
Ford
Foreman
Forman
Foster
Fox
Frances
Francis
Franklin
Frazier
Froe
Fryday
Fulsom

G
Gains
Garmon
Garrett
Gaskine
Gates
Gaylord
Geary
Gentry
Gibson
Gilbert
Glover
Golden
Gooden
Gordan
Graham
Grant
Gray
Grayson

Green
Gregory
Greyson
Griffin
Griggs
Grimmett
Guess
Gwin

H
Hamilton
Hammonds
Hampton
Hardgray
Hardridge
Harper
Harris
Harrison
Harrod
Harvey
Hasup
Hawkins
Hayes
Haynes
Henderson
Henry
Herod
Hershey
Higginbottom
Hill
Hills
Hobbs
Hodge
Holloway

Holmes
Homer
Hope
Horn
Houston
Howard
Hughes
Hunley
Hutton

I
Irving
Isaac
Isaacs
Island

J
Jack
Hackson
Jacobs
James
Jameson
Jamison
Jefferson
Minnerson
Joans
Job
Johnson
Jonas
Jones

K
Kanard
Kell

Kelley
Kelly
Kemp
Kennard
Kennedy
Kernal
Keyes
Keys
Kidd
King
Knowles
Krooms

L
Lacy
Lampkins
Landrum
Lawrence
Lee
Leffard
Lester
Lewis
Lincoln
Little
Logan
Loneon
Long
Love
Lovett
Low
Lowe
Lowery
Luckey
Lucy

Lunnon
Luster
Lyons

M
Mackey
Mahardy
Makins
Malvern
Malvery
Manac
Manuel
Marshal
Martin
Mathews
mayberry
Mayes
Mayfield
Mayson
McClain
McDaniel
McGee
McGilbray
McGirt
McHenry
McIntosh
McKellop
McKinney
McNac
McNack
McSims
Mcsims
Meriweatehr
Mike

Miles
Miller
Millett
Mimms
Minas
Minnis
Monday
Monroe
Moody
Moore
Morey
Morgan
Morris
Morrison
Mosley
Mullen
Mure
Murphy
Murray
Murrell
Murrill
Myers
Myles

N
Nail
Nash
Nave
Neal
Nero
Nevens
Nvins
Newell
Newman

Nichols
Nix
Noble
Norman
Norfer
Norwood

O
Olden
Oldham
Osborn
Osborne
Overton
Owen
Owens

P
Parker
Parlor
Paro
Patrick
Patterson
Payne
Pea
Perkins
Perry
Perryman
Peter
Peters
Peterson
Pettitt
Phillips
Pierce
Pippins

Poldo
Pompey
Pond
Ponds
Porlar
Porter
Post
Postoak
Potts
Pratt
Price
Primmer
Primous
Primus
Prince
Pyles

Q
Quabner
Quinn

R
Ragen
Ragsdale
Randolph
Rector
Redmon
Redmond
Redouth
Reed
Rentie
Rice
Richard
Richards

Riley
Roane
Robbins
Robertson
Roberts
Robertson
Robins
Robinson
Robison
Rodgers
Roe
Rogers
Rorex
Rose
Ross
Rowe
Russell

S
Samuel
Samuels
Sancho
Sanders
Sandy
Sango
Scales
Scott
Scruggs
Seaman
Sears
Segrip
Sells
Serrell
Sevel

Sewel
Sewell
Sharper
Shaw
Shawnee
Shelton
Shepard
Sherman
Shields
Shoals
Siah
Sier
Simmons
Simon
Sims
Skeeter
Smith
Sneed
Snowden
Solomon
Sookey
Sparks
Spencer
Spring
Stanford
Starr
Staten
Steadham
Stephens
Stepney
Stevens
Stevenson
Stewart
Stidham

Street

Stroy

Sugar

Sullivan

T

Tab

Tanner

Taylor

Tecumseh

Thomas

Thompson

Thursday

Tiger

Tipton

Tittle

Tobey

Tobler

Toliver

Tolliver

Tom

Toney

Trotter

Tucker

Turner

Typer

V

Vann

Vannoy

Vaughn

Verner

Vincent

Virgel

W

Wade

Walcot

Walden

Walker

Wallace

Wallas

Walton

Wamble

Ware

Warner

Warrior

Washington

Watson

Webber

Webster

Welch

Welsh

Wheat

White

Williams

Willis

Wilson

Wisner

Wofford

Wollard

Woodall

Woodard

Woodley

Woods

Wright

Y

Young

Seminole Surnames - Freedman and Blood Rolls

A

Aaron
Abb
Abey
Abraham
Adam
Adams
Ahaisse
A-ha-la-ko-
    chee
Ahaloke
Ah-ho-he
Ah-weep-ka
Albert
Ablerty
Alec
Aleck
Alecky
Alex
Alexander
Alfa
Alfred
Alice
Alicky
Allen
Alley
Allie
Amesta
Amey
Amos
Amy
Anderson
anna

Annie
Annoche
Archibald
Archockee
Archole

B

Baby
Baker
Barkus
Barnett
Barney
Barrisklow
Bean
Bear
Beard
Becky
Bemo
Bennett
Berry
Bettie
Betsy
Billy
Bottley
Bowlegs
Brown
Bruce
Bryner
Bryant
Buck
Buddy
Bull
Burden

Burgess
Butler

C

Caesar
Canard
Carbechochee
Carbiticher
Carolina
Carpitche
Carr
Carter
Carcher
Catchoche
Charlesey
Charley
Charlie
Charty
Checotah
Che-da-ka
Cheeska
Chepaney
Chepaney
Cheparney
Cheponoska
Chippee
Chisholm
Chochee
Choharjo
Chosey
Chotka
Chotke
Chotkey

Choya
Chulma
Chumsey
Chupco
Chupcogee
Church
Cindy
Clark
Cloud
Cobb
Co-e-see
Coffee
Coker
Coley
Concharty
Chondella
Condulle
Conhecha
Conner
Co-nok-kee
Contaley
Coody
Cooper
Cornelius
Cosar
Cotcha
Cowake
Co-wok-co-
 chee
Cox
Crain
Crane
Crow
Cudjo

Cudjoe
Cully
Cumpsey
Cumesh
Cundy
Cunny
Cunsah
Cynda
Cyrus

D
Daily
Dandy
Daniel
Davey
David
Davis
Davison
Dean
Deer
Dennis
Dicey
Dillsa
Dinah
Dundy
Dosar
Doser
Doyle
Dunford
Dunlap
Dyal
Dyer

E
Echoille
Edmond
Eliza
Ellen
Elochee
Elsa
Elsie
Elizabeth
Emartha
Emarthla
Emarthoge
Emmyu
Emoche
En-le-te-ke
Es-ho-po-na-ka
Estachukse-
 hoke
Estomethla
Eunasse

F
Factor
Fanny
Fay
Fekhoniyue
Fife
Fik-hith-ka
Fish
Fixico
Flanley
Foster
Fox
Freeman

220

Fulsom
Fuswa
Futchahoke
Futopeche

G
Gaines
Gano
Geroge
Gibbs
Gibson
Gibsy
Goat
Gooden
Gordon
Grant
Gray
Grayson
Greenleaf
Ground

H
Hagle
Haney
Hanna
Hannah
Hardy
Harjo
Harjoche
Harrison
Hatty
Hawkind
Hayecha
Hayes
Henne-ho-chee

Henny
Henry
Hepsey
Heshoka
Hill
Hilly
Hochifke
Hoktochee
Hoktoke
Holata
Holatka
Hollins
Holmes
Hopoille
Hotulke
Hulbutta
Hulhoke
Hulleah
Hully
Holwa
Hutke
Hutche

I
Ida
Iley
Ishmael
Island

J
Jacksey
Jackson
Jacksy
Jacob
JakeyJames

Janey
Jannati
Jefferson
Jemima
Jennetta
Jennie
Jesse
Jimmey
Jimmie
Jimmy
Jimpka
Jimpsey
Joanna
Jo-co-chee
Joe
John
Johnie
Jonoche
Johnsey
Johnson
Jonah
Jonasse
Jones
Joney
Josey
Joseph
Jushua
Judy
July
Jumper
June

K
Kamabe
Kane

221

Kaney
Katie
Katy
Kenah
Keno
Ke-pa-ya
Key
King
Kinnona
Kissie
Kith-lee
Kotska

L
Lanego
Larney
Lasley
Leader
Leah
Lelusse
Lena
Letka
Lewis
Lilwy
lina
Lincoln
Lindsey
Litka
Little
Lizzie
Losata
Lodie
London
Lopka
Lottie

Lotty
Louie
Louisa
Lousanna
Lovett
Lowe
Lowery
Lowesa
Lowiney
Lozana
Lucina
Lucy
Lula
Lumba
Lumsey
Lundo
Lusoche
Lustey

M
McCoy
McCulla
McGeisy
McGeisey
McGirt
McIntosh
McNac
Mahale
Mahardy
Malinda
Mandy
Maney
Manuel
Marcus
Maria

Marks
Marpiyecher
Marshal
Marshall
Martha
Marthla
Martin
Marty
Maryu
Matuth-hoke
Maude
Mecco
Meley
Melishkoche
Milisse
Milo
Megee
Meney
Mesale
Mesaley
Metetakee
Micco
Miley
Miller
Milley
Millie
Mills
Milly
Milsey
Mimey
Mina
Minda
Mingo
Misselda
Missena

Missey
Missie
Mitchell
Mitchile
Moloyike
Moleya
Mollie
Molly
Monacheke
Monday
Monkah
Mooney
Moore
Moppin
Morgan
Morris
Morrisona
Mosar
Moses
Mot-hoh-ye
Mulcussey
Mulcy
Mulgusse
Mulleah
Munday
Mungo
Munnah
Muthoye

N
Nancy
Nannie
Napoeche
Narcome

Natukse
Nellie
Nellsie
Nelly
Nelsey
Ne-ma
Nero
Nevins
Nicey
Nitchey
Nitey
Noah
Noble
Nokoseka
Nokusile
Nora
Noska
Nuksokoche

O
Okfuska
Okfuskey
Oksusky
Omayaye
Osborne
Othcchc

P
Palmer
Paney
Parney
Parhoche

Parnosa
Par-nos-co-che
Parsosee
Parnoskey
Paroah
Pssake
Pa-ta-ge
Payne
Pennose
Perryman
Peter
Phena
Phenie
Philip
Phillip
Phillips
Pheobe
Pilot
Pochuswa
Polly
Pompey
Ponkilla
Ponluste
Pon-no-kee
Porter
Possuk
Pottey
Powell
Proctor
Pollotka
Puncho
Punka
Punluste
Putken

223

R
Rabbit
Raiford
Reed
Renton
Renty
Rhoda
Riley
Ripley
Roberts
Roe
Rosanna
Ross

S
Sa-che-meche
Saketheche
Sakoeka
Sakteke
Saley
Salina
Salinda
Sallie
Sally
Saloche
Salma
Sam
Samby
Samele
Sammah
Sammy
Samochee
Sampson
Samuel
Sancho

Sandridge
Sandy
Sango
Sando
Sapallpake
Sapehunka
Sapkhohthe
Sarber
Sarney
Scipio
Scott
Seeley
Sefah
Seharney
Sehoka
Sehunka
Selba
Selda
Selma
Semissee
Sena
Se-ne
Sentevery
Sigler
Silla
Sillah
Semleteke
Simma
Silla
Sim-me-te-da-
  kee
Sim-e-di-ha-
  kee
Simena
Simon

Sisie
Sissy
Skiff
Smith
Solomon
Sona
Sonny
Sowanoke
Specneer
Stafey
Stanton
Steel
Stephenson
Stepney
Steppe
Stewart
Stedham
Street
Suc-car-see
Sullivan
Sumka
Sumpsey
Sunday
Sunny
Susanna
Susey
Susie
Suthoye
Su-wa-key

T
Tahike
Talmaswy
Talmacsy

Tanyan
Tar-co-sar
Tayeche
Taylor
Tecumseh
Teller
Tena
Te-tah-ke
Tewe
Thahoyane
Thasate
Thlocco
Thocco
Thomas
Thompson
Tiger
Tikahche
Ti-u-na
Tobie
Topche
Tomochusse
Tolomka
Tommy
Toney
Tulla
Tulsay
Turner

U
Ut-tleyh

V
Vann

W
Wadsworth
Waitey
Wakkie
Walker
Wallace
Walter
War-le-do
Warrior
Washington
Wasutke
Watson
Watty
Weattie
Webster
Weely
Wellington
Wells
Wesley
West
Wetley
White
Whitfield
Wildcat
William
Williams
Williamse
Willic
Willis
Wilsey
Wilson
Winey
Winton

Wise
Wisey
Wisner
Wirlow
Wright
Wyetka
Wolf
Wood
Wotko

Y
Ya-fo-la-gee
Yahola
Hakopuche
Yamie
Yanah
Yarber
Yarnah
Hekcha
Youney
Youngs
Yowelle

Appendix 4

Surnames of the Tri-Racial Families of the Upper South

Appendix 4

Surnames from the Tri-Racial Isolate Families

A
Adams
Adkins
Atkins
Allen

B
Bartlett
Bass
Bean
Bell
Benenhaley
Bennett
Berry
Bolen
Bowlin
Bowling
Boland
Bolton
Boone
Bone
Braboy
Braceboy
Braveboy
Bradby
Brewington
Bridger
Bright
Brigman
Brooks
Brown

Buckner
Bullard
Bunch
Butler

C
Carter
Chapman
Chavis
Chavers
Chavous
Chavez
Cole
Coleman
Collins
Cook
Cooper
Creel
Criel
Croston
Cumba
Cumbo
Comboes
Cummings

D
Dalton
Dorton
Dare
Delp
Denham

Dennis
Dial
Drake
Driggers
Driggus
Drighers
(Rodriggus)
Drinkwater

E
Emanuel
Epps

F
Fields
Freeman

Gabriel
Gann
Gibson
Gipson
Goen
Going
Goins
Gowen
Gowin
Gowing
Goodman
Gorvens
Graham
Grants

229

Broom
Groves

H
Haires
Hale
Harding
Harman
Harmon
Harris
Harvey
Harvie
Hatacher
Hawkes
Holmes
Hood
Howe
Hunt

I
Ivey

J
Jacobs
Jefferson
Johnson
Jones

K
Kennedy
Kitchen

L
Langston

Lasie
Lawson
Little
Locklayer
Lockalier
Locklear
Locklier
Lowry
Lucas
Locust

M
Mainard
Mainor
Maynor
Maloney
Manuel
Martin
Maynor
Miles
Miner
Minear
Mize
Moore
Moseley
Mullins
Melons

N
Nash
Newman
Newsom
Nichols
Noel

Norris

O
Oxendine

P
Page
Paine
Payne
Patterson
Perkins
Pinder
Pinoire
Powell
Price
Pritchard

R
Ransom
Ransome
Ray
Revels
Revil
Richardson
Roberds
Russell

S

Sammons
Sampson
Scholar
Scott
Sexton
Shavers
Shepherd
Smith
Stableton
Stevens
Stewart
Stuart
Sweat
Sweats
Sweet
Swett

T

Talley
Taylor

Terry
Thompson

V

Viccars

W

Weaver
White
Williams
Williamson
Willis
Wineoak
Winn
Wood
Woodson
Wott
Wynoak
Wynne

Appendix 5

Additional Black Indian Document Samples-

~Dawes Records

~Wallace Roll

~Kern-Clifton Roll

Index to the Dawes Rolls

Name	Roll No.	Name	Roll No.
Walker, Mary	601	Ward, Lilly	5179
Walker, Ruthu	935	Ward, Henry	5180
Walker, Jesse	967	Walls, Emily	890
Walker, Maria	968	Walls, Mary	3031
Walker, Mack	969	Walls, Zenolia	3032
Walker, Scott	970	Wand, Frances	802
Walker, Dickson	971	Walton, Beff	803
Walker, Leroy	972	Walton, Samuel	3747
Walker, Everetto	973	Walton, Sallie	3748
Walker, Alonzo	1701	Walton, Houston	3749
Walker, Velt	1702	Walton, Sam Jr.	3750
Walker, Jimmia	2499	Waldron, Celeste	1136
Walker, Oliver	5600	Waldron, Jesse	2127
Walker, Myrtle	2174	Waldron, George	2128
Walker, Dove	2175	Waldron, Henry	1142
Walker, Cole	2176	Waldron, Sophy	1143
Walker, Mabel	2177	Waldron, Jeff	3103
Walker, Ellen	1700	Waldron, George	5501
Walker, Amon	2178	Waldron, Harba	4246
Walker, Charles	2337	Wade, Aleck	1724
Walker, James	2403	Wade, Byington	1725
Walker, Mary	2790	Wade, Clayton	1726
Walker, Victoria	3072	Wade, Joshua	2350
Walker, Willie	3720	Waters, Robert	1748
Walker, Robert	4734	Waters, James	4337
Walker, Elizabeth	4756	Waters, Alfred	5333
Walker, Gertrude	4767	Watson, John	1752
Walker, Emma	4768	Watson, Maria A.	1753
Walker, Roxy Ann	4936	Wagoner, Columbus	1972
Walker, Emily	4956	Wagoner, Isom	1973
Walker, Oliva	4957	Wagoner, Annie	4908
Walker, Mary	4958	Walters, Ida	2045
Walker, Joe	5000	Walters, Celia	2441
Walker, Willie	5001	Walter, Louisa	2147
Walker, Lucinda	5002	Walker, Alemeta	4251
Warren, Jennie	283	Ware, Nancy	4383
Warren, Charlie	284	Ware, George	4827
Warren, Harriet	2239	Ware, Sam	4828
Washington, Bathya	431	Warner, Fred	4729
Washington, Lawyer	516	Walford, Henry	4791
Washington, Ann	517	Walford, Jimmie	4790
Washington, Mose	518	Wulford, Albert	4792
Washington, Effie G.	1583	Warrior, Angeline	4917
Washington, Caroline	2366	Webster, Manuel	28
Washington, Susan	2833	Webster, Lewis	30
Washington, Rosy	2834	Webster, Louisa	31
Washington, Lawyer	2835	Webster, Troy	5168
Washington, Harvey	2836	Wellington, Jerry	511
Washington, Laurinda	3247	Wellington, Mariah	730
Washington, Ada	3325	Welch, Jimmie P.	4743
Washington, Rebecca	4068	Webb, Sylvia	5307
Washington, Elizabeth	4118	Webb, Chester	7308
Washington, Clayburn	4119	West, Ella	5445
Washington, Sarah	4120	White, Edmond	1654
Washington, Ida	4131	White, Louisa	1759
Washington, Charley	4122	White, Beatrice	1800
Washington, Melvina	2307	White, Ether	2164
Ward, Harman	923	White, Forbus	2168
Ward, Sampson	1831	White, Bennie	2201
Ward, Solomon	1832	White, Eddie	2202
Ward, Monroe	1833	White, Curtie	2203
Ward, Mattie	1834	White, Lonnie	2205
Ward, Emma	1835	White, Clemmie	2231
Ward, Amos	1836	White, Bessie	2236
Ward, Edmund	1837	White, Nancy	2241
Ward, Willie	1838	White, Dewey	2242
Ward, Birdie	1839	White, Fannie	5014
Ward, Mary	2059	White, Mary	5260
Ward, Walter	2134	White, Jim	5262
Ward, Margie	2211	White, Napoleon	5263
Ward, Lillie	2216	White, Naomi	5264
Ward, Henry	2715	White, Frank	5266
Ward, Susan	2734	White, Bertha	5396
Ward, Howard	3614	White, Irving	5478
Ward, Hattie	3615	White, Sam	5478
Ward, Melia	3616	White, Robert	5489
Ward, Sloan	3632	White, Lilly	5524
Ward, Jane	3633	White, Harry	5525
Ward, Jennie	3534	Whitaker, Patsy	2921
Ward, Sophia	5176	Whitaker, Irene	2923
Ward, Jesse	5177	Whitaker, Elvira	2924
Ward, Tandy	5178	Whitby, Alex	5199
		Williams, Ida	14

This is the official page from the Final Roll of Choctaw Freedmen, that reflects the Walton family on the Dawes Roll. Their roll numbers appear to the right.

The Dawes Enrollment Card

This is the Dawes Enrollment card of the Walton family.
They were enrolled on Freedman card No. 777. The tape
used to repair the card has darkened the image in places.
The name of the Choctaw slave owners is reflected on the
card. Other freedman cards from the various nations are
similar to this card in design and information. The family
applied for enrollment in June of 1899 and was finally
approved in 1904, as reflected on the stamp at the bottom left
of the card.

Application Jacket: Dawes Interview

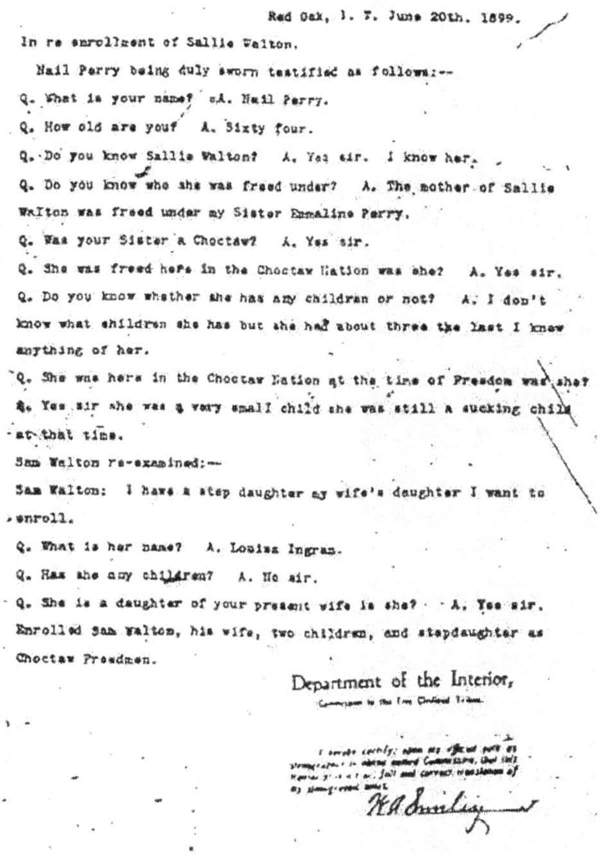

Red Oak, I. T. June 20th, 1899.

In re enrollment of Sallie Walton.

Nail Perry being duly sworn testified as follows:--

Q. What is your name? A. Nail Perry.

Q. How old are you? A. Sixty four.

Q. Do you know Sallie Walton? A. Yes sir. I know her.

Q. Do you know who she was freed under? A. The mother of Sallie Walton was freed under my Sister Emmaline Perry.

Q. Was your Sister a Choctaw? A. Yes sir.

Q. She was freed here in the Choctaw Nation was she? A. Yes sir.

Q. Do you know whether she has any children or not? A. I don't know what children she has but she had about three the last I knew anything of her.

Q. She was here in the Choctaw Nation at the time of Freedom was she? A. Yes sir she was a very small child she was still a sucking child at that time.

Sam Walton re-examined:--

Sam Walton: I have a step daughter my wife's daughter I want to enroll.

Q. What is her name? A. Louisa Ingram.

Q. Has she any children? A. No sir.

Q. She is a daughter of your present wife is she? A. Yes sir.

Enrolled Sam Walton, his wife, two children, and stepdaughter as Choctaw Freedmen.

Department of the Interior,

This is an image from the Application Jacket M1301 where the Waltons were interviewed in front of the Dawes Commission. It is part of the interview from the case study in chapter 6. Interviews vary in length from as few as 1 page to dozens of pages, in some cases.

Indian Agent John Wallace conducted the Wallace Roll, in the late 1880s. The Cherokee Nation eventually discarded the roll, however, it is quite useful in finding ancestors on a roll prior to the Dawes Roll. The information on this roll reveals the name, age, and Cherokee Nation District of each enrollee.

337. Minerva Weber (daughter)   F. 20. Coowoesscowoo.
338. Davis Weber (son)   M. 18. "
339. David Weber (son)   M. 16. "
340. Georgian Weber (daughter)   F. 15. "
341. George Henry Weber (son)   M. 15. "
342. Eliza Weber (daughter)   F. 9. "
343. Anna Weber nee Sanders (daughter-in-law)F. 22. "

344. Willis Rogers,   M. 40. "
345. Sarah Rogers (wife)   F. 30. "

346. Dick Whitmire,   M. 72. "
347. Walter Whitmire (same as Mattie)   M. 19. "
348. Emma Whitmire (daughter)   F. 12. "
349. Charles Whitmire (son)   M. 14. "

350. Sarah Murrell,   F. 56. Saline.
351. Maggie Murrell, (daughter)   F. 25. "
352. Susan Murrell (daughter)   F. 23. "
353. George Murrell, (son)   M. 21. "
354. Daisy Murrell (daughter)   F. 18. "
355. Allen Rogers (son)   M. 34. Coowoesscowoo.
356. Sim Rogers (son)   M. 36. "
357. Sallie Rogers (Granddaughter)   F. 13. "
358. Ioonage Rogers, (grandson)   M. 9. "
359. Rosa Rogers (granddaughter)

The Kern-Clifton Roll created in 1896 was to add information that was omitted by the Wallace Roll. Both were later put aside by the Cherokee Nation, but again this is another roll that might prove useful genealogically.

The samples of documents on the previous pages are presented primarily to reflect the enormous wealth of data that can be obtained in a variety of documents.

The serious researcher will want to employ as many primary documents as possible in the genealogical search.

It is imperative that the genealogical researcher maintains a separation between the content found within the documents and the political motivation behind the creation of the documents. These were created from a political circumstance that did not have genealogists in mind, so some of the questions that might arise for many persons will not always have immediate answers. Objectivity, of course is the basis of all sound research. Hopefully these sample documents both Federal census and the specialized Freedman records, will provide an avenue of research for the genealogists wishing to explore his or her Black and Indian family history.

Bibliography

For African-Native American Research

Bibliography

Abel, Annie Heloise. The American Indian as Slaveholder and Secessionist. Cleveland: Arthur H. Clark Company, 1915.

Bateman, Rebecca Belle. "'We're Still Here'": History, Kinship, and Group Identity among the Seminole Freedmen of Oklahoma." Ph. D. diss., Johns Hopkins University, 1991.

Braund Holland, Kathryn E. "The Creek Indians, Blacks and Slavery," Journal of Southern History 57

Burton, Art T. Black, Red and Deadly. Black and Indian Gunfighters of Indian Territory Austin TX, Eakin Press 1991

De Marce, Virginia Easley. "Verry (sic) Slighty Mixt. Tri-Racial Isolate Families of the Upper South." National Genealogical Society Quarterly, March 1992 p. 6-35.

Flickinger, Robert Elliott. The Choctaw Freedmen and the Story of Oka Hill Industrial Academy. Fonda, IA: Journal and times Press, 1914.

Gammon, Tim. "Black Freedmen and the Cherokee Nation." Journal of American Studies 11 (December 1977): 357-364.

Halliburton, R., Jr. Red Over Black: Black Slavery among the Cherokee Indians. Greenwood Press, 1977.

Littlefield, Daniel F. Jr. Africans and Seminoles. Westport, CT: Greenwood Press, 1977.

Littlefield, Daniel F., Jr., and Mary Ann Littlefield. "The Beams Family: Free Blacks in Indian Territory." The Journal of Negro History 41 (January 1976): 17-35.

Littlefield, Daniel F., Jr. Africans and Creeks. Westport, CT: Greenwood Press, 1979.

Littlefield, Daniel F., Jr. The Cherokee Freedmen. Westport, CT: Greenwood Press, 1978.

Littlefield, Daniel F., Jr. The Chickasaw Freedmen. Westport, Ct: Greenwood Press, 1980.

Miles, Tiya, The Ties that Bind. The Story of an Afro-Cherokee Family in Slavery and Freedom Berkeley and Los Angeles: University of California Press Ltd. 2005

Miles, Tiya, Holland, Sharon, editors, Crossing Waters, Crossing Worlds. The African Diaspora in Indian Country Durham & London, Duke University Press, 2006

Mulroy, Kevin, The Seminole Freedmen, A History, Norman: University of Oklahoma Press, 2007

Mulroy, Kevin, Freedom on the Border: The Seminole Maroons in Florida, th Indian Territory, Coahuila, and Texas Lubbock Tex. 1993

Katja May, African Americans and Native Americans in the Creek and Cherokee Nations, 1830s to 1920s: Collusion and Collision (New York: Garland Publishing, Inc., 1996)

Perdue, Theda. <u>Slavery and the Evolution of Cherokee Society, 1548-1866.</u> Knoxville: University of Tennessee Press, 1979.

Saunt, Claudio, <u>Black, White and Indian. Race and the Unmaking of an American Family</u> Oxford, New York: Oxford University Press. 2005

Strauss, Terry ed., <u>Race, Roots & Relations Native and African Americans.</u> Chicago: Albatross Press, 2005

<u>Voices of Indian Territory</u> Terry Ligon and Angela Walton-Raji, editors. Vol 1, No. 1 Catonsville MD, 2005-2008

Walton-Raji, Angela Y., <u>Black Indian Genealogy Research. African American Ancestors Among the Five Civilized Tribes.</u> Bowie MD, Heritage Press, 1993

Works Projects Administration <u>Slave Narratives. A Folk History of Slavery in the United States, from Interviews with Former Slaves.</u> Vol. 6. Oklahoma & Mississippi (St. Clair Shore Michigan: Scholarly Press 1976)

Wright, J. Leitch, Jr. <u>Creeks and Seminoles: The Destruction and Regeneration of the Muscogulge People</u>. Lincoln: University of Nebraska Press, 1986.

Wright, J. Leitch, Jr. <u>The Only Land They Knew.</u> New York: The Free Press, 1981.

Zellar, Gary <u>African Creeks. Estelvsti and the Creek Nation</u> Norman: University of Oklahoma Press, 2007

Index